TEACHING
STEM
LITERACY

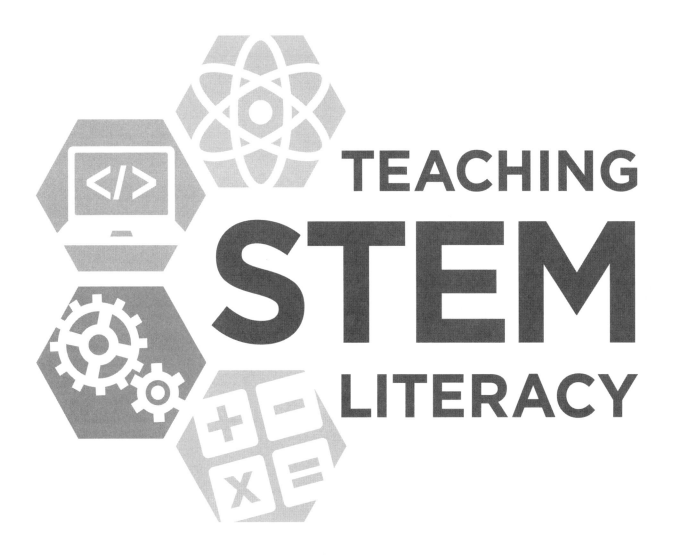

TEACHING STEM LITERACY

A Constructivist Approach
for Ages 3 to 8

JULIANA TEXLEY

RUTH M. RUUD

Redleaf Press®
www.redleafpress.org
800-423-8309

Published by Redleaf Press
10 Yorkton Court
St. Paul, MN 55117
www.redleafpress.org

© 2018 by Juliana Texley and Ruth M. Ruud

First edition 2018
Cover design by Erin Kirk New
Cover image by arrow-stock.adobe.com
Interior design by Ryan Scheife, Mayfly Design
Typeset in the Whitman and Gotham typefaces
Interior illustrations by Lauren Cooper
Printed in the United States of America
24 23 22 21 20 19 18 17   1 2 3 4 5 6 7 8

Library of Congress Cataloging-in-Publication Data
Names: Texley, Juliana, author. | Ruud, Ruth M., author.
Title: Teaching STEM literacy : a constructivist approach for ages 3 to 8 /
   Juliana Texley, Ruth M. Ruud.
Description: First edition. | St. Paul, MN : Redleaf Press, 2017. | Includes
   bibliographical references.
Identifiers: LCCN 2017011980 (print) | LCCN 2017023060 (ebook) | ISBN
   9781605545639 (ebook) | ISBN 9781605545622 (paperback)
Subjects: LCSH: Science—Study and teaching (Early childhood)—United States.
   | Science—Study and teaching (Early childhood)—Methodology—United
   States. | BISAC: EDUCATION / Teaching Methods & Materials / Science &
   Technology. | EDUCATION / Preschool & Kindergarten. | EDUCATION /
   Curricula. | EDUCATION / Teaching Methods & Materials / Mathematics.
Classification: LCC LB1585.3 (ebook) | LCC LB1585.3 .T483 2017 (print) | DDC
   372.35/044—dc23
LC record available at https://lccn.loc.gov/2017011980

Printed on acid-free paper

Dedication

This book is dedicated to the thousands of teachers who have inspired and encouraged our work—who work with creativity, energy, and empathy to bring all children to their personal best. In the past few years, we have had the pleasure of collaborating with many talented educators, who have generously shared their insights and practical tips with us.

Thanks also to our husbands, who have helped us as we've worked with these educators. We have traveled the United States and the world, and they've always been alongside us, supporting science education in their own ways.

And, of course, we dedicate this book to children everywhere who are empowered by their STEM adventures. These explorers are our future. May their endless questions keep us young!

Contents

Acknowledgments

We would like to thank the following people for their contributions to this book:

Peggy Ashbrook, whose The Early Years column and liaison work with the National Association for the Education of Young Children assists National Science Teachers Association members.

Vicki Cobb and all the other authors who share their muses with us.

Alicia Conerly and Kristin Poindexter for reviews, photos, and inspiration.

Suzanne Flynn, coordinator of NSTA Recommends, for great trade book suggestions.

Linda Froschauer, who has guided NSTA's *Science and Children* to include rich resources for early childhood teachers.

Carrie Launius, who helped NSTA redefine STEM literature.

Page Keeley, whose expertise on formative assessment is known across the United States.

Christine Royce, who is a true guide in the choosing and using of trade books.

Introduction

Starting with STEM

Children are born curious. They are scientists and engineers from the first time they reach out to explore their world. As they grow, they ask many questions each day about the world around them. This is how children build confidence, capacity, and mental habits that will enable them to conquer the challenges of their futures and ours.

As early childhood educators and caregivers discuss education today, they often use the acronym STEM to refer to an integrated approach to science, technology, engineering, and mathematics. STEM is more than a list of content, concepts, and skills. It's a holistic approach to educational experiences. STEM practices provide pathways to discovery from babyhood through adulthood. But as you will see from the discussions that follow, even the acronym STEM can be limiting. It may lead teachers and caregivers to create artificial lines between ways of knowing. We need to remember that discovery also involves reading, communicating, social skills and studies, music, and the arts. Discovery seldom falls into any single category.

Early investigations begin in very personal ways. In the language of educators, learners observe phenomena. That's a term that simply means anything that catches their interest! Phenomena spark questions, and questions lead to investigations. At the early childhood level, STEM practices like observing, questioning, modeling, and communicating are purposeful play. As children build confidence, they use these practices to find personally meaningful solutions to the problems they encounter. They design experiments, collect information, test and retest, and communicate what they've found. We adults can analyze these activities all we want. But to young children, they are simply natural behaviors with significant benefits to their habits of mind and their sense of competence.

A Basis in Research

Much of what we do in STEM education is built on the seminal work of twentieth-century researchers. In the 1930s, American psychologist and educational reformer John Dewey developed an instructional model based on a philosophy he called the "complete act of thought." He wrote that to begin a sound educational experience, students must sense something that perplexes them and then act on it. Three decades later, Swiss psychologist Jean Piaget explored cognitive development in children. He emphasized the importance of physical experiences in learning, from a child's earliest years. From the 1960s onward, educators moved from a pedagogy based on direct instruction (teaching things) to constructivism (creating learning environments that let children examine their own preconceptions and construct their own knowledge, yielding far more meaningful and lasting ideas than children acquire by simply being told things).

"Constructivism" is a term that might seem complex and mysterious to those who are not involved in education research. But once you know what it means, the concept is both simple to understand and easy to identify. In the 1970s, researchers tried to determine what successful programs and methods had in common. The researchers found that the common element was not what happened in the classroom but what the teachers and caregivers believed about learning. If the adults thought they were the providers of information, they were not successful. If they believed that children needed to build ideas on their own, magic happened. This book is built on that paradigm. Even though it outlines a foundation of core ideas, the path to those ideas is always through the explorations of the learner.

In the 1980s, education researcher Rodger Bybee and his associates at the Biological Sciences Curriculum Study developed an instructional model called the 5Es. Since then, this framework has become the most familiar sequence for planning lessons with a constructivist approach. The 5E framework involves the following phases:

- engagement

- exploration

- explanation

- elaboration

- evaluation

This model is based on a strong body of research (Bybee et al. 2006). Many studies have demonstrated that this approach increases the growth of logical reasoning and engagement at every age. A major summary of the field, published by the National Research Council (NRC), summarizes learners and learning as follows:

- Students come to the classroom with preconceptions about how the world works.

- To develop competence in an area of inquiry, students must have a foundation of factual knowledge, understand facts and ideas in the context of a conceptual framework, and organize knowledge for retrieval and application.

- Teachers help students learn to take control of their own learning by defining goals and monitoring their progress in achieving them (NRC 1999).

The 5E model is much more than a mnemonic for making lesson plans. It is a framework for teaching and learning. We *engage* with the phenomena that interest students. Then we allow learners to examine their own preconceptions by *exploring*. This is a very important step. Without examining what we think we know, those ideas persist. *Explaining* can help learners organize their observations. Explanations don't always come from the teacher or caregiver. In fact, it is often best practice to just wait and listen. Children truly benefit from explaining to one another.

Elaboration connects the phenomena that have been explored in the classroom to authentic real-world contexts. This transfer of understanding makes learning relevant. It also offers a great opportunity for transfer of ideas from the early childhood program to the home. This book includes messages to families so that children's conversations about phenomena can continue.

The process of *evaluation* is often misunderstood in STEM education. It involves both learners and their guides—evaluation of both learners and the learning environment. Although it is listed last of the 5Es, evaluation must be ongoing. It's important to think of this phase not as a test but rather as a sort of sensor to help us move forward, backward, or roundabout. Early childhood teachers and caregivers are really the experts here; they understand that open dialogue is one of the most powerful tools of evaluation at this level. Veteran teachers may be surprised at the broad and eclectic approaches to evaluation suggested later in this book. But we believe that those who guide young children in exploration have antennae better than any assessment system available.

Building on History

In 1996 the NRC formulated the *National Science Education Standards* (NSES). This document brought together much of the research and practice that had come before. But it was limited in its pedagogy. It clustered content in three- to four-year blocks beginning with kindergarten, with little detail on progressions. It left to educators the job of sequencing content within those blocks. After a decade of slow implementation, educators looked for more. We can look back today and see how this process and its products might have been improved. Nonetheless, this first national codification of what children should learn in science strongly influenced the profession by emphasizing the need to coordinate content with process, teaching, assessment, and program- and system-level support.

In 2012 the NRC released *A Framework for K–12 Science Education*. This effort by scientists, psychologists, and educators formulated a powerful vision of science and engineering education. It defined a pedagogy of "three-dimensional learning," which integrates the methods (practices) of science and engineering, content, and broad concepts that cut across all disciplines. The *Framework*'s implementation document, published in 2013, is called the *Next Generation Science Standards* (NGSS).* The 2013 NGSS differs from the 1996 NSES in four important ways:

- Whereas NSES grouped goals by elementary school, middle school, and high school, NGSS defines clear, research-based learning progressions for each grade level.

- NSES was written in a one-dimensional way. It emphasized the importance of process (inquiry) in standards separate from the content goals. NGSS summarizes the end goals of each area as three-dimensional performance expectations, saying that practice and content are intrinsically intertwined with conceptual learning.

- NGSS emphasizes crosscutting concepts, which are repeated again and again across time and learning spaces. Ideas such as energy, scale, and size or structure and function can be applied to many experiences and areas of the curriculum.

- NGSS content is written in a very different way from NSES content. For example, a "disciplinary core idea" in NGSS may include the types of evidence that might be used in activities rather than simply the conclusions to which scientists might arrive. From the earliest levels, learners are encouraged to explain not just what they think but why they think it.

The following table shows an example of the different ways in which NSES and NGSS approach the same learning goal.

---

* "Next Generation Science Standards (NGSS)" is a registered trademark of Achieve. Neither Achieve nor the lead states and partners that developed the Next Generation Science Standards were involved in the production of this product and do not endorse it.

NSES-NGSS Comparison

National Science Education Standards (1996)	Next Generation Science Standards (2013)
As a result of the activities in grades K–4, all students should develop • abilities necessary to do scientific inquiry • understanding about scientific inquiry As a result of the activities in grades K–4, all students should develop • understanding about position and motion of objects	K-PS2-1. Plan and conduct an investigation to compare the effects of different strengths or different directions of pushes and pulls on the motion of an object. K-PS2-2. Analyze data to determine if a design solution works as intended to change the speed or direction of an object with a push or a pull. 3-PS2-1. Plan and conduct an investigation to provide evidence of the effects of balanced and unbalanced forces on the motion of an object.
(NRC 1996)	(NGSS Lead States 2013)

The content listed in this table's two columns may seem parallel on the surface. But whereas NSES describes the end result of processes, NGSS describes the processes themselves. The latter approach leads to more active questions and invites learners to launch their own investigations.

Veteran teachers may be asking what happened to the ubiquitous word "inquiry," which guided so much of curriculum development for so many years. The concept of inquiry still exists in NGSS. But in NSES, it was vague, almost impossible to assess, and in many ways frustrating. By contrast, NGSS's Science and Engineering Practices define very specific skill sets that we use to inquire, investigate, and develop solutions.

Thinking of all these historic milestones in education as a progression, not as separate paths is essential. Moving from one level of understanding to the next never means abandoning the wisdom of the past. As Piaget wrote about cognitive schema, educators all over the world were observing them. Bybee and other leaders used the constructivist learning theory that was being implemented in classrooms all over the United States. And many of the same people who crafted NSES in the 1990s worked on the *Framework*. Meanwhile, most teachers were already creating many three-dimensional educational environments. The *Framework* recognized this and provided a body of research and best practice on which educators could rely to build more such environments. Tomorrow's early childhood STEM education will enrich what we have today, not replace it.

Early childhood teachers and caregivers should recognize in the *Framework* and NGSS the positive things they are already doing. Then they can use these documents to do even greater things. While the documents do not specifically discuss the prerequisite skills necessary at levels before kindergarten, it is easy to also connect this pedagogy to habits of mind like persistence, curiosity, and logical thinking. Questioning, finding patterns, classifying, and engaging in argumentation are embedded in almost all early childhood programs.

NGSS leaders and the National Science Teachers Association (NSTA) have supported the development of more active STEM curricula for early childhood. In fact, NSTA has developed a joint position statement on early childhood science education with the National Association for the Education of Young Children (NAEYC) that represents another first. Here a just a few of the points made in that statement:

- "Children have the capacity to engage in scientific practices and develop understanding at a conceptual level." It is never too early to explore science.

- "Adults play a central and important role in helping young children learn science." These adults include not only teachers but also caregivers and parents, in a rich partnership that emphasizes exploration and experience without requiring extensive content knowledge.

- "Young children need multiple and varied opportunities to engage in science exploration and discovery." While the prospect of integrating science into most early childhood experiences may seem daunting at first, it is really just an enrichment of what is normally done in school and child care settings (NSTA 2014).

Educators are celebrating the increased prominence and significance of STEM experiences at the early childhood level. That's because these experiences are so naturally integrated into our understanding of what's appropriate at that level. It's also because early childhood professionals share the joy of that discovery every day.

Sample Early Childhood Experiences That Prepare Young Learners for Scientific and Engineering Practices

Practice	Performance	Sample Experiences
Asking questions	Learner can distinguish between questions that can be tested and questions that can't.	After observing children on a swing, learner asks whether heavier children swing longer or faster.
Designing experiments	Learner compares and collects data.	Comparing heavy and light swingers, learner realizes the push must be fair to be measured.
Developing models	Learner understands that a small sample of a phenomenon can be like a larger, real-world sample.	Learner looks at different areas of the school yard, some with plants and some without, and realizes that plants help prevent puddles.
Using data	Learner connects real-world observations and symbols.	Learner maintains weather data to decide whether special clothing will be needed.
Communicating information	Learner shares understandings that were developed by observations and supports claims with evidence.	Learner provides arguments, advice, or other communications based on observations to help others stay safe or comfortable.

Critical Thinking

When young learners bring their thousands of questions to early childhood programs, it's vital that adults don't ask children to leave those questions at the door. Making space for critical thinking in an early childhood environment can be a challenge. It takes time and patience—even when we've spent the better part of an evening planning for the day's experiences. If the children come to school with a completely different agenda for learning, we need to take a step back and just enjoy the trip.

In her book *Teaching Emerging Scientists*, teacher-educator Pamela Fraser-Abder encourages us to make a primary goal of fostering learners who do the following:

- continually seek to know and understand

- question all things

- interpret all available data

- base judgment on evidence

- respect logic

- consider the consequences of their actions

- demonstrate intellectual independence (Fraser-Abder 2011, 5)

These expectations are intrinsic to the STEM approach. They also provide the foundation for differentiating a STEM classroom for the needs of all children. Be prepared. Critical thinking can lead learners to surprising questions. Never be afraid to say, "I don't know; let's find out together."

Reading the Framework and NGSS in an Early Childhood Context

The *Framework* and NGSS define an extensive set of progressions in practices, concepts, and content that includes all the academic disciplines. Some early childhood educators consider this structured approach to expectations (what children should be able to do) somewhat daunting, especially when added to the language arts and mathematics expectations that increasingly crowd K–2 programs.

But when early childhood teachers and caregivers look deeper, they almost always discover that they are already doing most of the groundwork for these expectations. Even if the language of the *Framework* and NGSS is a bit different, the practices are easy to recognize in existing programs. Early childhood education is intrinsically integrated; guides know that it is not appropriate to divide curricular time into subjects. The science goals are treasures buried within what we already do.

NGSS's content (called Disciplinary Core Ideas) may seem new to early childhood teachers and caregivers upon their first read. This is particularly true in the physical sciences. Traditionally, when teachers at this level have taught science at all, they have tended to emphasize the life sciences. Yet the physical and earth sciences often come more naturally to very young explorers. Their days are full of pushes and pulls, forces and motion, and sensory experiences that help them identify the properties of matter. Water and weather provide the scientific raw materials for all sorts of investigations. Every adventure young children undertake is filled with the sorts of questions and observations that lead to understanding and problem solving. Although these areas have been underemphasized both in preservice teacher education and in supporting materials like trade books, they are great areas for integrated exploration.

NGSS emphasizes crosscutting concepts that span all disciplines and all lessons. The key to teaching and learning crosscutting concepts is making connections. That is a challenge. Connecting a fall unit on force and motion to spring activities in gardening and nutrition takes some creativity. And connecting a classroom experience to "homework" that families can share, as described on page 3, may require creativity, too. But children are surprisingly open to such connections. The following table offers some examples of questions that connect crosscutting concepts in early childhood:

Sample Crosscutting Concepts in Early Childhood

Crosscutting Concept	Questions That May Lead to Conceptual Understanding
Cause and effect: mechanism and explanation	What makes things move? Why do things fall? What slows down motion? How does energy change a substance? Why are there always puddles under the swings?
Energy and matter: flows, cycles, and conservation	Where does energy go as an object moves? How does energy change the surface of the earth? What is a food chain? What kinds of homes stay cool in the summer?
Scale, proportion, and quantity	How can we separate things that are heavy and light? Why does water get bigger when it becomes ice? Why does a big animal need to eat more than a small animal? How big will the plants in my garden be when they are grown?

Many teachers and caregivers believe that they must totally abandon their traditional topics in order to accommodate the *Framework* and NGSS. That's not true. But it is true that we must reconsider how and why we teach these concepts as we move toward more three-dimensional STEM education. For example, dinosaurs are a common topic because they have great tongue-twisting names and can be big and scary. But we need to think deeply about what important concepts we can learn from dinosaurs. They are perfect for illustrating the relationship between structure and function. (How is the bony frill of a stegosaurus like the big ears of an African elephant?) Dinosaurs can also be used to study scale, proportion, quantity, and the flow of energy through food chains.

STEM Education and the Common Core

Traditional teacher education programs have prepared many teachers to think that language arts, mathematics, and the sciences can be taught separately. Today we know better. The questions children ask about the phenomena that fascinate them do not tolerate boundaries. That's why early childhood education is integrated, with no boundaries between disciplines.

But how does this integrated approach align with the curriculum standards to which many schools and early childhood programs adhere? Let's take a look at some of those standards. Most K–12 schools today have aligned their mathematics and language arts curricula to the Common Core State Standards (CCSS). These research-based standards begin at kindergarten, but many pre-K experiences serve as building blocks. Consider these CCSS expectations for kindergarten:

CCSS.ELA-Literacy.SL.K.3

Ask and answer questions in order to seek help, get information, or clarify something that is not understood (CCSS Initiative 2016a, 23).

CCSS.ELA-Literacy.SL.K.4

Describe familiar people, places, things, and events and, with prompting and support, provide additional detail (CCSS Initiative 2016a, 23).

CCSS.ELA-Literacy.SL.K.5

Add drawings or other visual displays to descriptions as desired to provide additional detail (CCSS Initiative 2016a, 23).

CCSS.Math.Content.K.MD.B.3

Classify objects into given categories; count the numbers of objects in each category and sort the categories by count (CCSS Initiative 2016b, 12).

Then look at the Scientific and Engineering Practices for K–12 Science Classrooms in *A Framework for K–12 Science Education*:

- asking questions (for science) and defining problems (for engineering)

- developing and using models

- planning and carrying out investigations

- analyzing and interpreting data

- using mathematics and computational thinking

- constructing explanations (for science) and designing solutions (for engineering)

- engaging in argument from evidence

- obtaining, evaluating, and communicating information (NRC 2012, 42)

Finally, look even further. Here are Standards for Mathematics Practice from CCSS:

- Make sense of problems and persevere in solving them.

- Reason abstractly and quantitatively.

- Construct viable arguments and critique the reasoning of others.

- Model with mathematics.

- Use appropriate tools strategically.

- Attend to precision.

- Look for and make use of structure.

- Look for and express regularity in repeated reasoning. (CCSS Initiative 2016b, 10)

CCSS encourages questioning, communicating, and using observations (data) to argue for ideas. The *Framework* and NGSS include very similar goals, such as (in mathematics) analyzing data and using mathematics and computational thinking, and (in language arts) constructing explanations, engaging in argument, and communicating. These are all appropriate from the earliest years onward.

Each area of NGSS includes careful correlations to CCSS. In fact, some observers have called this approach to STEM education "Common Core on steroids." That is why it is important to recognize that *Teaching STEM Literacy* is not a diversion from basic language arts and mathematics goals; rather, it is a faster and more efficient path to achieving them. In appendix D at the end of this book, we've added just a few of the many research studies to support this claim—ammunition for anyone who hears that there is "no time for STEM."

The Elements of STEM Education

⬢ Beginning with Science

While the elements of STEM are inherently integrated, many people associate STEM education first with science. That's because the authentic explorations children love often have a science context. Families associate STEM programs with science, too. The phenomena that we use as lures for learning are most easily linked to science literature.

The following units suggest many books that explain simple science concepts (disciplinary core ideas) in authentic and often humorous ways. For example, children can look at their toys through the eyes of a classic scientist in Lynne Mayer's *Newton and Me*. Or they can laugh at the antics of Wile E. Coyote in Mark Weakland's *Thud!* while learning about friction. With science books, it's hard to resist the temptation to read from cover to cover. But as you'll see in the examples in each unit, the most direct path toward understanding often isn't a straight line. Begin at the beginning, in the middle, or at the end. Stop whenever you want to try out ideas or to ask questions. Read a section twice. Leave a great book at a learning center for later fun. Reading science should be verbal, kinesthetic, and motivational. As children listen or read, allow them to use all their other senses. Stop for work (investigation) or play (the same thing!). And create spaces where children can explore for a while then read again.

🛑 Using Technology Thoughtfully

Technology comes naturally to today's "iGen"—the generation that has never known a world without smartphones, tablets, and constant access to the Internet. They take for granted gadgets that seem new to grown-ups. There was once a time, not too long ago, when educators believed that young children could not learn real things in virtual environments. Today's iGen proves that idea false. A lot of learning can occur in the virtual contacts that surround young children today.

But along with the technology ideas we provide in this book, we add a caution. Early childhood software and technologies are everywhere. It's tempting to grab for convenient software products or websites that say they can teach. But remember, young children must still construct ideas through authentic, physical experience first. They must also have opportunities to relate their physical experiences to virtual simulations in a progressive and developmentally appropriate way. Then we can use technology as a bridge between real and virtual worlds. The key is to use good judgment and select developmentally appropriate tools. In this book, we've recommended websites in which the simulation software is ideal for the developmental level of young children and easily linked to the real world.

In the context of an early childhood STEM curriculum, technology can be simple—much simpler than a smartphone, tablet, or virtual game. A measuring tool like a trundle wheel, a spring scale, a clicking metronome, or a thermometer might be exactly what a child needs to quantify observations. A wide ribbon can become the pathway to understanding a computer-created graph. A camera can be the tool through which little scientists communicate big ideas.

Some of the books in appendix A (Science Books for Children) have a heavy emphasis on technology. For example, *Hello Ruby: Adventures in Coding* by Linda Liukas describes the most basic concepts underlying computer programming as the natural investigations of a child. Other books involve technology throughout, such as *Sydney and Simon: Full Steam Ahead!* by Paul

Reynolds. Because technology is so ubiquitous in the lives of our children, calling children's attention to the tools we use is sometimes helpful.

Ⓔ Engineering Is Exciting

In many curricula, the "E" in "STEM"—engineering—is the newest and least explored element of STEM education. Engineering is using nature's energy and resources to fill needs, solve problems, and achieve goals. Early childhood engineering experiences should involve problems that are authentic to young learners—questions about things in the children's immediate experience. The possibility of solving a child's own problem often lights the fire in a STEM lesson. Something needs to be fixed! Or a new way of doing things must be invented! Watch carefully and you will catch the youngest learners engineering solutions to simple problems, such as building play structures or designer foods. The problem that starts the STEM experience can come from home, classroom, a great book, or even the Internet. That's why STEM is a state of mind, not just a loose amalgam of content areas. The ability to use STEM skills and ideas to make a child's personal world better empowers children to become problem solvers in larger contexts.

But there are still far too few engineering opportunities in most early childhood programs. If they exist, they are often limited to building ideas (civil engineering) or inventions and placed at the end of a unit. That's where we've put engineering ideas in this book, strictly as an organizational device. But they don't have to be there and, in fact, often work better at the start of a unit. In addition, we've tried to broaden our engineering ideas to include agricultural engineering and safety.

In your work with young children, don't neglect to point out engineering practices in fields other than buildings and infrastructure. For example, gardening (see unit 12 on page 145) presents the same sorts of opportunities for design, evaluation, redesign, cooperation, and persistence that are inherent in constructing a building or testing a bridge.

Veteran teachers and caregivers may recall the so-called scientific method from their own education and training. Of course, there are many scientific methods, and the methods of engineering are even more appropriate to early childhood. Early childhood teacher educator Angi Stone-MacDonald and her colleagues summarize an engineering experience in these steps:

1. Think about it.

2. Try it.

3. Fix it.

4. Share it. (Stone-MacDonald et al. 2015, 6)

Stone-MacDonald and her coauthors explain how the engineering process of "universal design" applies well to creating STEM environments for young children. In building a physical environment, an architect might try to achieve a facility that every person can enjoy. In the classroom, universal design sets the following goals:

- providing multiple means of representation or choices for perception

- providing multiple means of action and expression

- providing multiple ways of engaging students (adapted from Stone-MacDonald et al. 2015, 24)

In this way, educators who want to nurture young engineers become engineers themselves.

These steps are parallel to and compatible with the 5E model we described earlier. Demonstrating thinking is both communication and formative assessment. What's different here is the idea that an engineering adventure is seldom done. Testing, retesting, and never giving up are STEM skills. Several of the books we've recommended speak to this. They may not seem like traditional science books at all, but they emphasize the practices of engineering and the habits of mind that lead to successful problem solving.

Children are often engineers first (looking for solutions to problems they encounter) and scientists later, in order to understand those problems. By its very nature, engineering requires repeated attempts; there is no failure, only persistence. And engineering requires teamwork, a natural skill to encourage in young children. As defined by NGSS, engineering goes far beyond building structures. Every problem or puzzle has the potential for an engineered solution. The STEM approach implies not only content but also application. In this sense, engineering isn't a subject or a discipline; it's a process and a mindset. It allows learners to assign purpose to their investigations. They begin by recognizing a problem and go on to produce products about which they can be proud.

The books in our units that best illustrate engineering are often subtle and intriguing. Ashley Spires's *The Most Magnificent Thing* provides a striking example of the practices that make inventors succeed: relevance, design, redesign, persistence, and creativity. The lead character has an idea, but to create her magnificent thing, she needs patience (which she sometimes lacks), persistence, creativity, and hard work. This sort of book is a great accompaniment to the engineering challenges in our units. Use science, but think like an engineer. Build a better shoe or toy or garden in your own environment!

Ⓜ Math Is Everywhere

Many early childhood teachers and caregivers have limited background in science content yet still infuse curiosity and joy into their lessons. But these same teachers are sometimes puzzled by the emphasis on mathematics in the *Framework*'s core ideas and crosscutting concepts. They are often really quantitative. Here are just a few examples of areas where math is an essential part of science exploration:

- Environmental studies include population counts, energy measurements, and climate data.

- Studies of properties of matter include measurable ideas about temperature, weight, and inertia.

- Studies of force and motion include ways to measure speed, distance, time, and vectors.

The good news is that there are opportunities to use math every day in every way. But teasing out the connections takes time. Textbooks and published curricula don't provide as many connections as early childhood teachers may need. The level of the mathematics required to understand, represent, or investigate an idea may not match precisely the CCSS or the school district's curriculum. That's particularly true when children are investigating their own questions. They often stretch beyond their age or grade level for the mathematics skills they need. To collect data for an argument or an invention, they may need to explore different kinds of measurements, algorithms, or graphs. That's half the fun!

When you are planning a STEM curriculum for young children, check out the correlations provided by the Next Generation Science Standards resources (see appendix D). We've provided a few suggested CCSS connections in the book, but there are so many more. Remember that exploring children can stretch for the math (and language arts) skills they need to answer the questions they've developed. Mathematics is both a tool for STEM and a resource.

Each unit in this book involves some mathematics understanding. Most often it is measurement. Keep in mind that what we want children to understand is that things *can be measured*. It doesn't matter whether children time their slide rides with a stopwatch or a metronome. However they measure, they are being scientists.

We've also included some great examples of mathematics books that encourage children to observe in nature—especially to observe patterns. For example, Sarah C. Campbell's two books *Growing Patterns: Fibonacci Numbers in Nature* and *Mysterious Patterns: Finding Fractals in Nature* encourage nature observation at all age levels. Other books show STEM activities that intrinsically involve mathematics.

STEM Plus: Social Studies and the Arts

It's easy to see that there are powerful social studies lessons in the pages of this book, too. Here are just a few of the "Themes of Social Studies" published by the National Council for the Social Studies (NCSS) that fall easily into a STEM curriculum:

- Children in early grades learn to locate themselves in time and space.

- During their studies, learners develop an understanding of spatial perspectives and examine changes in the relationship between peoples, places, and environments.

- Young children learn how science and technologies influence beliefs, knowledge, and their daily lives (NCSS 2010).

We've also used art and music throughout this book. We want to make sure that we address not just minds but also hearts.

STEM Plus: Social Learning

Every early childhood program places significant emphasis on social learning skills. STEM is the ideal context in which to embed these goals. In the book *Engaging Young Engineers: Teaching Problem-Solving Skills through STEM*, Angi Stone-MacDonald and her coauthors provide a clear and research-based justification for this approach: "Collaborative thinking is the primary 'social ingredient' of problem-solving, and its importance cannot be overstated. Few real-world problems are solved by a single individual. Instead, groups and teams of individuals must work together effectively, asking questions, pooling information, contributing to and critiquing concepts and jointly testing solutions" (2015, 136). The authors point out that many of NAEYC's key early childhood program standards are effectively met through collaborative STEM problem solving. Here are just two examples:

1.D.05.d. Ensure that each child has an opportunity to contribute to a group (NAEYC 2015, 6).

1.F.02.b. Guide and support children to play cooperatively with one another (NAEYC 2015, 8).

Researchers have found that the STEM approach not only encourages social learning but also is especially effective for students who might be less able to integrate into a regular classroom. STEM provides a relevant context for English-language learners, students with behavioral challenges, and those with developmental delays. We've accumulated a few sources of this research in appendix D.

Assessing Progress

The "evaluate" step in a 5E STEM lesson can be the most challenging. In NGSS, the content, concepts, and practices of STEM are summarized in performance expectations for children in kindergarten and older. These three-dimensional challenges can direct our attention to goals that are far broader than just something that should be learned on a given day. At the preschool level, the habits of mind that are building blocks for STEM learning are often evident in growth in communication, observation, and questioning skills.

Peggy Ashbrook, who contributes an ongoing column called The Early Years to NSTA's elementary journal *Science and Children*, offers some expert observations about assessment in her book *Science Learning in the Early Years: Activities for PreK–2*. She writes that we must "recognize that young children are developmentally ready to build on and revise their knowledge" (2016, 40). Ashbrook warns that to assess, however, early childhood teachers must be "prepared to collect evidence of thinking, ability, and understanding" (41). Her book offers a complete outline of key behaviors that show understanding, an assessment tool based on deep understanding of the varied and sometimes inconsistent signs of achievement that young children might provide.

A significant innovation in the formulation of the NGSS performance expectations is the common inclusion of "assessment limits." We include many experiences in a three-dimensional lesson that are meant to be building blocks to future learning. We do not need to "test" every idea or skill every time. In fact, many of the understandings that we introduce in early childhood will not be developed to the extent that they could be tested for many years. So an assessment limit clearly tells the educator that children are building foundational understandings that won't fully be tested until much later.

Many teachers' guides also include "right answers" to all the questions we pose to children. You won't find much of that in this book. Yes, we have included some content background and teacher tips so that you won't go too far astray in guiding children's exploration—and, of course, so that you'll feel comfortable exploring on your own, since you are a lifelong learner. But in many cases, we've noted that any logical answer that comes from a child's own experience is the right one. Certainly, any answer that can lead to another question and another exploration is the best one of all.

Children can learn to be self-evaluators through creative metacognition. That means they benefit from thinking about their own thinking. Dialogue is the key to helping this happen. In this area, some of the most important work today is being done by Page Keeley, whose book series Uncovering Student Ideas in Science has influenced both assessment and instruction across the nation. Keeley offers quick formative assessments, which she calls "probes," to allow teachers to take the pulse of a class and individual students. The probes are usually common situations with carefully designed choices based on what we know about levels of student understanding. We've included one of her probes from *Uncovering Student Ideas in Primary Science* on page 53.

Probes are not tests in the traditional sense. They are meant to be mile markers on the exciting road to STEM ideas. In most cases, they consist of a dialogue that might show a variety of children's explanations for common phenomena. Constructed from a deep understanding of typical misconceptions, probes can help a teacher or mentor evaluate a child's understanding of claim, evidence, and reasoning and can produce great scientific argumentation in young children. They are a natural way for early childhood teachers and mentors—who are almost always expert listeners—to focus their listening in order to get a better idea of what children are thinking. We encourage you to explore this method of uncovering the ideas of your own students.

Of course, formal probes like the one we've reprinted are not the only sorts of assessments that should occur all the time in the early childhood STEM environment. Teachers and caregivers can encourage drawing, sharing, and showing off. Digital cameras are ubiquitous today; they offer a great way to meld technology and assessment. And just listening to the buzz in a room can be the most effective assessment of all.

Never Too Young for STEM

While NGSS begins at kindergarten, it is clear that younger children enjoy and benefit from early experiences with STEM content and the practices of science and engineering. In each chapter, we've included a few ideas for younger children as they explore the basic core ideas. (Look for the sidebars titled Early Explorers.) While their understandings may be inconsistent, these first "experiments" with the world around them are very important. They build not only skills but also confidence. They are never too young to begin. But remember, these are not goals that should be assessed except in the most general way, as prompts for good conversation.

The Importance of Physical Science

NGSS includes a tightly constructed set of learning progressions built with a strong reliance on learning research. While it's rewarding to have freedom to choose from a variety of topics in an early childhood classroom, research shows that ideas need to be both spiraled and connected to be understood. It's not good practice to organize topics by teacher interest or long-stored materials. For example, in NGSS you'll find a disciplinary core idea about forces and motion for kindergarten, and you'll see that same idea again in grade two. The language may look similar at both levels, but the depth of understanding will progress, and the suggestions for assessment will become more refined.

Similarly, discussion about properties of matter begins in grade one and progresses through middle elementary.

Following those progressions, a concept that is introduced (but not assessed) in kindergarten might be reinforced again in grade two as children's logical and analytical skills mature. Many of the activities in this book's units have that capacity and room for teachers to adapt and modify the lessons not only for several grade levels but also for accelerated learning. There is ample room for individualization, modification, and adaptation for diverse learners and learning environments, too. The activities provide many paths to help learners bloom through STEM. There is also a continuum of content, concepts, and skills in the higher grades with notes to show the connections. Peer tutoring experiences can be easily designed, pairing upper grade students with early childhood investigators.

Most importantly, each of the lessons is built around the philosophy of purposeful play that has been shown to be best practice for early childhood. The lessons are meant to be fun! And they involve no more specialized equipment, experience, or preparation than would be available to most early childhood leaders all over the country. Each section of the book that follows is meant to lead children to the greater confidence and capacity that a deep understanding of our world brings. To paraphrase the words of STEM evangelist Ainissa Ramirez, in children's future travels, we want them to be pilots, not merely passengers. We want them to be prepared to play future games we can only imagine (2014).

Choosing and Using the Best Literature

Integrated within each unit of this book are one or more national award–winning trade books. Since 1973 the NSTA has collaborated with the Children's Book Council (CBC) to identify a list of Outstanding Science Trade Books for children. The term "trade book" simply means "not a textbook." The emphasis of a trade book is on reading for enjoyment and exploration. Trade books are almost never leveled readers, but the reading level of each book that we have cited is appropriate for most learners in the primary years.

Outstanding science books are not just accumulations of facts. Rather, these books invite students to use the practices of science. The lure can be the questions, the illustrations, or the models used by researchers. Accurate facts are important, but practices and concepts are even more important. NSTA provides online lists of these exemplars going back to 1996 and publishes the new list each March for educators and media specialists. Each of these books provides opportunities for children to observe, to analyze, to explore, and ultimately to communicate about science.

In the past few years, educators have come to realize that STEM literature is different from science literature. STEM literature often integrates several areas—science, technology, engineering, and mathematics. But integration isn't the primary criterion. There may be almost no disciplinary content at all. STEM literature invites exploration and problem solving without boundaries. So in 2016, NSTA and CBC launched a new project, developed in partnership with other STEM groups—the International Technology and Engineering Educators Association (ITEEA), the American Society for Engineering Education (ASEE), and the Society of Elementary Presidential Awardees (SEPA)—to create a separate list called Best STEM Books. These award-winning books inspire inquiry and excitement using all STEM disciplines and those habits of mind that contribute to STEM success.

What characterizes the Best STEM Books? In the words of the first joint committee, they invite STEM thinking by doing the following:

- modeling real-world innovation

- embracing real-world design, invention, and innovation

- connecting with authentic experiences

- showing assimilation of new ideas

- illustrating teamwork, diverse skills, creativity, and cooperation

- inviting divergent thinking and doing

- integrating interdisciplinary and creative approaches

- exploring multiple solutions to problems

- addressing connections between STEM disciplines

- exploring engineering habits of mind, such as systems thinking, creativity, optimization, collaboration, communication, and ethical considerations (Launius 2017)

The Best STEM Books represent the practices of science and engineering by doing the following:

- asking questions, solving problems, designing, and redesigning

- integrating STEM disciplines

- showing the progressive changes that characterize invention and/or engineering by demonstrating designing or redesigning, improving, building, or repairing a product or idea

- showing the process of working through trial and error

- progressively developing better engineering solutions

- analyzing efforts and making necessary modifications along the way

- illustrating that failure might happen and that is acceptable, provided that reflection and learning occurs (Launius 2017)

Meeting these criteria is a tough challenge. Yet in the list's first year, the joint committee found many current books that fit the bill. The honorees for the first year (2016) with special relevance in early childhood are included in appendix C. It's important to note that many of these books do not seem to contain much disciplinary content (science, mathematics, or engineering facts). Instead, the books invite children to find those elements on their own.

An ongoing column in NSTA's journal *Science and Children* is Teaching Science through Trade Books. One of the column's authors, Christine Anne Royce, contributed a chapter to a book on early childhood STEM by Linda Froschauer, *Bringing STEM to the Elementary Classroom*. Royce's chapter is titled "Design Dilemmas." One of the books she cites exemplifies the difference between a science book and a STEM book for early childhood: *The Most Magnificent Thing* by Ashley Spires (see page 14). Royce writes that the character in the book "demonstrates the trial, error, perseverance, and adaptation aspects of the design process" (Froschauer 2016, 19). That's not traditional science; it's engineering, and it is a great way to emphasize those habits of mind with young children. That's why STEM books have an important place in the early childhood classroom.

STEM Schools

More and more, learning communities are aspiring to become STEM schools. But as professionals have gathered at STEM conferences, it has become apparent that there are diverse definitions of STEM schools. In many places, the process of becoming a STEM school begins with a simple coordination of lessons and ideas among the four STEM fields. Enhancing that coordination by connecting language arts, social studies, and the fine arts comes next.

But to truly implement STEM pedagogy, learning communities know that they must eliminate the lines between subjects entirely, as we've explained above—and that's really hard to do. To understand the difference, think about the definition of a STEM trade book (as opposed to a science book) above. The words that come up most often are "invite" and "innovate"—representing an attitude that encourages any kind of question and all sorts of pathways to answers. STEM schools invite innovation.

To emphasize the importance of integrating across subjects and grade levels, great STEM schools celebrate programs guided by questions. There are common themes, and children move from room to room and from grade to grade carrying the same STEM attitude. Visually and through the curriculum, STEM schools often emphasize claim, evidence, and reasoning (CER). From the earliest years onward, the conversation sounds like this: "Oh, that's an interesting thing you said. Why do you think that's true? Did your senses tell you? Can you explain your idea more?" This sort of approach leads to a consistent pedagogy.

Whatever content building blocks a school community chooses to implement in a STEM environment, keep in mind that the most important mortar is integration. STEM has no boundaries, and neither should your explorations. Learning to see from the perspectives of those who explore through varied ways of knowing is the key.

Teaching STEM Literacy: A Guide to Using This Book

In the pages that follow, teachers and caregivers will find twelve developmentally appropriate units for STEM physical and earth science in early childhood. Each unit is aligned with one or more of the K–2 performance expectations in the *Framework* and the corresponding practices, content, and concepts for specific grade levels in NGSS. For children in the preschool years, these experiences are easily modified to build the readiness skills that will serve them well as they grow. (An Early Explorers sidebar in each unit explains how to modify it for pre-K.) Each experience is meant to encourage and affirm children's abilities of observation, questioning, and data collection. At the early childhood level, these experiences should be considered small steps on the exciting pathway to STEM. The lessons combine discovery, problem solving, and engineering solutions to authentic questions that young children might ask. They offer opportunities to collect data, using mathematics skills to support scientific arguments. The lessons also provide natural links to award-winning literature, to provide the seamless integration that early childhood educators find most natural. Most importantly, they are intended to foster communication skills.

This book isn't meant to be a how-to book. It's an invitation. The best questions for a STEM lesson are the ones that come in the door with the child. But starting every day anew wouldn't be practical in any educational setting. You can create enticing phenomena, or *engage,* in ways that allow you to predict and prepare for at least some of the questions in advance. That engagement might begin with a demonstration, a great read, a video of a familiar phenomenon, a walk around the school, or just a collection of interesting things in a center. Exploring any of these paths will provide somewhat predictable phenomena for children.

Each unit begins with a core idea, includes readable explanations, and provides general directions. Of course, we've already stipulated that when the unit begins with curiosity, it may not be possible to predict exactly where the adventure will end. It's important to realize that the step-by-step approach in each unit is only meant to be an initial road map. You don't have to know what's around each corner to enjoy the journey. The most interesting paths may not be the ones we suggest but the ones that children themselves forge. So we hope that every reader will enjoy the freedom to adapt and modify every idea here to suit the early childhood classroom, informal environment, or community setting where learning is happening. The activities included in each unit can be changed easily to fit not only children's interest and ability, but also the facility, the schedule, and the curriculum.

Each unit is designed to illustrate three-dimensional learning, emphasizing practice, content, and concept and leading to an engineering or problem-based experience. We acknowledge up front that no single unit can accomplish everything we'd like. NGSS was built on the assumption that learning progresses over time. Only a long view of a child's accumulated investigations would fully illustrate all the dimensions of learning implied in our understanding of best practice. So we do not include checklists of every practice or concept that might be touched by each set of activities. Teachers and caregivers should feel free to follow the natural curiosity of their students.

Sidebars in the lessons show samples of alignments to CCSS for language arts and mathematics. A far more complete list of potential CCSS correlations is available at the NGSS website and in its publications. These references will be especially valuable for classroom teachers who want to demonstrate that "starting with STEM" is a research-based way to achieve standards in literacy and mathematics in an efficient and authentic way. We encourage readers to refer to the rich resources accumulated by Achieve for NGSS (see appendix D) for a more complete index.

Each lesson also includes activity guides. Although these may look like worksheets, they are simply models for dialogue and for conducting the activities with a variety of age levels. Key vocabulary words are noted in bold type. While we have provided some matrices for recording data, paper is not always necessary. You might replicate the data sheet on a whiteboard or other display device. But there are some situations in which paper becomes valuable. When an activity is linked to a note sent home with children, the data sheet can be a nice supplement so that some part of the activity can be replicated or extended.

Each unit has a vignette of a scientist or inventor, titled STEM Star. These vignettes are not meant to be history lessons. A STEM star is a role model for the practices of science and engineering and for the habits of mind that empower investigators and innovators. Read the book *The Inventor's Secret* by

Suzanne Slade for clues about those traits. You won't find out how to build a car in this book. You will find out what Thomas Edison advised Henry Ford: "Keep it up!"

Both the activity guides and the STEM Star vignettes of scientists and engineers may be above the reading level of some young STEM explorers. If appropriate, peer partners can be ideal for these activities. Another way to respond can be with audio-recording devices.

Finally, to make full use of the ideas, you may need to cover up the clock. Don't fall into the trap of saying, "There's no time for science." Strong research supports the idea that language arts and mathematics skills come faster when embedded in relevant explorations of authentic science and social studies (NRC 2011). Because the practices of science include rich experiences in language arts and mathematics, there's no time to skip them!

What You'll Need

The average early childhood environment is not designed as a traditional science lab. But most environments are designed for purposeful play, and that's perfectly adequate for STEM learning. The lessons that follow will not require a great deal of equipment and will be easily accommodated in almost any early childhood setting.

Physical science is the essence of play. And fortunately, the typical early childhood setting has many tools children can use for this purpose—sand and water tables, playground equipment, blocks and other building toys. NGSS's Disciplinary Core Ideas for physical science in the primary years are the same ideas that propel balls, wagons, swings, and sliding children. Earth science content contains a significant physical science component, plus the properties of familiar substances. Even if the content background of many great early childhood teachers and caregivers doesn't include a lot of physical science, that's easy to remedy. Not only have we provided quick content briefs here, but great resources can be found online. One is the collection of Science Objects in the NSTA Learning Center (http://learningcenter.nsta.org/products/science_objects.aspx). NSTA's e-book *Force and Motion* provides not only content but also pedagogy and links to common childhood misconceptions that are very valuable when designing instruction.

When you are looking for STEM learning equipment, don't forget families. We've provided some suggested notes to families that include requests for common materials. Change the notes as needed for your situation. Making families partners in touring through garage sales and end-of-season clearance sales is a great way to increase enthusiasm for STEM.

BASIC EQUIPMENT

Unit 1: Pushes and Pulls You'll need playground equipment, cameras, and timing equipment. An old, loud metronome is a good tool here. Spring scales are available from science suppliers. Sometimes these scales are used to weigh fish, so they may be available at stores that sell fishing equipment. Spring scales may also be available at cooking stores. Having a few of the toys that are illustrated in Lynne Mayer's *Newton and Me* (such as wagons and balls) for demonstration and conversation will make the literature integration come naturally. A camera and printer (to make photos of students as they use playground equipment) are optional. For the engineering challenge, you'll need cameras (or phones), a way to print photos on paper, and labels.

Unit 2: Falling Down You'll need objects that can fall without endangering children, such as beanbags or clay figures, syrup or molasses; a collection of objects of about the same size but different masses, such as keys and coins, Ping-Pong balls and golf balls, rectangular sponges and crumpled paper. You might also want a rug sample, rubber pad, or car mat so that the objects do not break on impact. Have unbreakable items available, such as a bar of soap, a sponge, a shoe, rubber bands, a scale, and molasses to drip into a cup. This will make the book come alive for the children. For the engineering challenge, you'll need an egg carton and eggs. Use a bathroom scale or spring scale to limit the size of the container and create a fair test.

Unit 3: Heavy and Light You'll need two small plastic containers per group (identical in size with opaque, different-colored lids); more pairs of objects, such as small and large washers, blocks, or small toy figures; pairs of kitchen sponges of the same size and shape; access to water; pieces of plywood, paneling, or plastic (about eighteen by six inches); and triangular blocks or other objects for use as fulcrums. For the engineering challenge, you'll need soft model "hooks" made of pipe cleaners or bendable plastic, two feet of string for each group, a variety of small objects (heavy and light) that can be attached to the string, paper clips, and a source of water for testing the inventions. If you don't have an empty aquarium, your custodian or cook may have a sink deep enough to help with this. Toy fish for the bottom of the pool add to the fun.

Unit 4: Rolling, Rolling, Rolling You'll need a ramp (U-shaped molding or toy ramp), balls and other objects of similar size that might go down the ramp quickly or slowly, measuring tools, markers or wide ribbon to indicate the end of the roll, and sticky notes. For the engineering challenge, you'll need materials to build a ramp, tape, paper, measuring tools, and small disks such as checkers, quarters, or washers to tape to toy cars. Samples of helmets (such as bicycle and baseball helmets) can help reinforce safety concepts as you read about and discuss this unit's STEM star.

Unit 5: Slipping, Sliding You'll need a metronome with an audible click, a playground slide, and waxed paper. For the extension, an older child volunteer might bring a skateboard and a helmet. A piece of rough wood and a piece of tile or plastic the same size can be used as a platform to pull books or toys. (The material used to make a balance in unit 3 might be ideal.) For the engineering challenge, you'll need the ramp from unit 4; waxed paper or spray wax; small objects (ideally plastic models of shoes, which are often sold as fobs for key rings) with a flat, smooth surface; and materials to make the bottom surface rougher, such as tape, glitter, or sand.

Unit 6: What's the Matter? You'll need cylindrical glasses, ice cubes, nonlatex gloves, water, a variety of winter gloves and mittens, and measuring instruments (graduated cups and a scale). For the engineering challenge, you'll need more gloves, measuring instruments, ice, and thermometers.

Unit 7: Drop by Drop You'll need water droppers, water, towels, small plastic dose cups or ketchup cups for measuring, a hand mirror, a variety of containers that may or may not hold water (sieves, colanders, pans, paper cups and bowls, sponges, empty cans without sharp edges), waxed paper, dish soap, thermometers (plastic or metal-backed for safety), ice, salt, and food coloring. To make Barton's book more exciting, use a large squirt gun. For the engineering challenge, you'll need sets of cans, one "soda" size and one slightly larger, and materials to test for packaging, such as paper, sawdust, Styrofoam peanuts, rag strips, and thermometers.

Unit 8: It's in the Air You'll need bubble wands, bubble soap, clear plastic cups, clear soda, raisins, small balloons, clothespins, wire hangers, paper forms cut to look like helicopters, and paper clips. For the engineering challenge, you'll need paper airplane materials, scissors, tape, and paper clips.

Unit 9: Sun and Shadow You'll need light sources (such as flashlights), various shapes that correspond to characters or to your mathematics curriculum (circles, squares, triangles), a variety of transparent and translucent materials (pieces of plastic, sheer cloth, and so on), sunlight-reactive beads, ice cubes, and sunscreens. To prepare for the gardening activities in unit 12, you'll need a map of the school grounds or a community area with familiar markings, such as big trees and playground equipment. For the engineering challenge, you'll need an object that can be set up as a sundial (any tall, thin object with a base), sidewalk chalk, and flags or bits of clay to mark shadows.

Unit 10: Hot Stuff, Cool Science You'll need two identical character toys, thermometers (either the kind that contain colored alcohol with safety backing for children or the forehead strips used for taking children's temperatures), a camera, and photos of children clothed for warm and cool weather. If available, you can use an infrared thermometer or temperature gun (available for less than twenty dollars at hardware stores), to measure temperatures. For the engineering challenge, you'll need boxes cut in house shapes, thermometers, paints, and a variety of roofing materials (such as cloth, Styrofoam, grass, and rubber).

Unit 11: Wind and Water You'll need photos of erosion, cameras, table pans or disposable paint pans, clean sand or soil, cups with small holes that can be used to make rain fall on the sand or soil, and straws. For the engineering challenge, you'll need the same pans and sand or soil, and cups with holes, plus plants, rocks, and other materials that might be used to slow erosion.

Unit 12: Growing Engineers Because this garden project can vary widely by region and by the physical circumstances of your environment/program, the list of materials needed will vary, too. You will begin with maps, cameras, and other resources for students to plan. To mark out how large a plant might grow, lids from large frying pans are easy to handle. Of course, you'll need seeds, small shovels, and watering cans. When it's time to actually create your garden, rely on your families and your community. In almost every state, the cooperative extension service (usually affiliated with your state's land-grant university) has a master gardener program. The graduates of this program would probably love to help you.

Classroom Management and Safety

Early childhood teachers often rival military generals in their ability to create and manage classroom environments. They understand that developmentally appropriate practice (DAP), as defined by NAEYC and other organizations, is not only the key to effective learning but also provides safer experiences. Extensive discussion of DAP is available at the NAEYC resource included in appendix D at the end of the book.

We could never anticipate every hazard that an activity might entail, but we have provided notes in each unit with cautions about common risks. Above all, it's important to keep these principles in mind for every activity:

- Keep developmental levels in mind. An activity that might be fun for a middle elementary child might be confusing and dangerous at an earlier level. Sometimes peer activities can complicate this issue because more children with varied levels of understanding are in the same small space.

- Post and review clear, short safety rules for each part of each activity. Some have been noted in sidebars in the text. In other cases, you may wish to add rules that are relevant to your own circumstance. Drawings or photos of safe practice are ideal.

- Space is key. If your group is large or your workspace is small, ask for help to divide the group or exchange spaces for the activities.

- Think about breakage and disposal in advance.

- Try the activities yourself first, imagining that you are your least predictable child.

- Limit the time for each section of the activity. A general rule is that children will not concentrate for more minutes than their years of age. Break activities into small parts, with time for conversation, reflection, and regrouping between parts.

- Build in accountability. Many of the activities ask children to stop to draw, write, record, or photograph. These natural bridges help maintain control.

- Help children structure time and space with visual or auditory cues. A musical signal might mean "come up front" or "cleanup time." Predictability is a component of safety.

- Eye protection is always recommended whenever investigators use (any) chemicals, or there is risk of impact or particles. Wash the goggles in antibacterial soap water between uses.

- Outside activities may provide more space for all that youthful energy, but there are risks outdoors, too. Playgrounds require specialized design for safety.

- While most early childhood programs include times and places for healthy eating, we've avoided doing experiments with materials that could also be eaten in the science space. Always distinguish science equipment from snacks. This is important, because as children's science experiences broaden, we don't want them to confuse something from an experiment with something that's for lunch. Unit 2 offers suggestions for looking at food packaging. Do these dropping activities in an area that is easily cleaned and hasn't been used for experiments. If you want to check cookie packaging and eat the cookies, too, do the activity in the cafeteria.

- Encourage responsibility by asking children to be part of the setup and cleanup. But never ask children to retrieve or store a stock of any chemical (even vinegar or baking soda) that might be harmful.

- Always let common sense rule.

Using Literature Links

Each unit in this book follows a standard scheme. It starts with guiding question and a quick summary of the core idea, followed by a 5E lesson outline, literature links, and an engineering challenge. But the reading can come any time—just as the lesson might begin rather than end with engineering. It is important to integrate literature throughout a lesson, not just as an introductory experience or a culminating practice. In some units, a book begins the adventure; in others, it continues the adventure or provides some closure. Teachers and caregivers should feel free to vary the way in which they integrate literature. And, of course, don't put those books away. In a center or reading nook, children will access books again and again.

The recommended literature for each unit includes both outstanding science books and samples from the new Best STEM Books list. While many older books that were once considered science books are appropriate for STEM integration, teachers and caregivers may have to use them in different ways. That means opening them up as invitations rather than as conclusions.

Probably the least effective way to share a great sample of children's literature is by reading it from beginning to end, isolated from an experience. The first book we've featured, *Newton and Me*, is full of photos and examples of toys. It would be a shame to ignore those invitations to exploration. In *I Fall Down*, author Vicki Cobb shows all sorts of things dropping. Drop that book and play!

And, of course, don't read the books just once. Put a book in a station, with lots of objects to manipulate and experiment with.

Like all great magicians, early childhood teachers and caregivers know that their patter is important. Many of the books that we have recommended model the sort of dialogue that encourages the development of questions and argumentation intrinsic to science practice. Open-ended questions like those in the Try It! and STEM Stars activities make an experience much more valuable. We cannot always take children out of the classroom to extend their explorations. For an excellent discussion of modeling using literature, see the video "Developing and Using Models of Electrical Interactions" at www.teachingchannel.org/videos/teaching-science-with-books-nsf.

Unfortunately, because physical science has not been emphasized as much as it should have been in the publishing industry over the past few years, some of the books we've listed are old and may be hard to obtain. For a special collection of the best science and STEM books published over the past decade and a half, visit www.nsta.org/publications/ostb.

Pushes and Pulls

The Big Question: What Makes Things Move?

Creating Context

What makes things move? In the simplest sense, an unbalanced force makes something move—makes it change position, speed up, or slow down. In this unit, children learn that they can measure the physical evidence of forces acting on objects. The key forces we'll discuss are pushes and pulls.

Prepare for the unit by emphasizing simple key vocabulary in advance. For example, say, "I am going to **push** the computer cart to the back of the room," or "Can you help me **pull** the door shut?" Post these terms on a word wall and ask children to use them when appropriate. Ask families to use the words at home, too. Using key terms in a deliberate way is a good way to motivate young scientists. But beware: science isn't a foreign language. Keep the number of new words to a minimum.

Engage

Introduce pushes and pulls by making small, age-appropriate toys available. At the earliest levels, trucks and wagons are simple enough to stimulate explorations. You can also use toy trains, car and ramp systems, and spring toys, such as a jack-in-the-box. In an environment where many manipulatives are stored, you might begin with a scavenger hunt, asking children to find toys that they can push or pull. Encourage verbalization as you review. Assign children to **pull** a wagon full of books to the library or to help a cafeteria worker **push** the milk cart.

You can enhance this introductory experience with technology. Provide cameras so children can find and document people pushing or pulling. Or use the Internet to find photos, and have children select those that show pushes and pulls.

Disciplinary Core Ideas

PS2.A: Forces and Motion

- Pushes and pulls can have different strengths and directions. (K-PS2-1, K-PS2-2)
- Pushing or pulling on an object can change the speed or direction of its motion and can start or stop it. (K-PS2-1, K-PS2-2)

Performance Expectation

Students who demonstrate understanding can:

Analyze data to determine if a design solution works as intended to change the speed or direction of an object with a push or a pull. (K-PS2-2)

(NGSS Lead States 2013)

TEACHER TIP

A swing is essentially a pendulum. If the push is the same, the number of swings will be the same, because this number is determined by the length of the rope or chain, not by the size or weight of the swinger. But the point of this activity is to help children realize that forces can be measured and to have young learners feel and discuss those pushes and pulls. In early childhood, the exact mechanisms for movement of a child on a swing or a bob on a pendulum are not relevant. The takeaway from the exploration should be that a force (a push) makes the swinger move away from the earth, and another force (gravity) pulls the swinger back toward the earth.

Remind the children not to pump their legs as they swing. Say, "Sit still on the swing." That's the only way to make this a fair test. The torque, or rotational force, provided by pumping leg muscles complicates the physics of the experiment.

Encourage students to think about the forces that oppose the push in this activity. Gravity is just one of them. (You can explore gravity further in the next unit.) Wind resistance also slows the swinger. So does friction where the swing is attached to an overhead beam or bar. Children can feel the wind resistance but not the friction.

Explore

Take a field trip to the swings. Ask one child (ideally, an older peer) to give a single push to another child. Count how many swings (forward and backward) the child gets with no leg pumping before the swing stops. Older children can also collect data using a clipboard.

Repeat the activity with different children. Is the result about the same? Create a chart that lists the swingers in two groups: big children and small children. Do big children swing more times after one push than little children do? Repeat the activity with the adults on the swing. Remind children that to be fair, the push must be the same. Use the same child as a pusher and the same amount of force in every trial.

What happens if you push harder? Repeat the activity with a single hard push. Make sure it is a fair test.

Explain

Pushes and pulls are forces. Other forces oppose pushes and pulls. When the swinger goes up, gravity pulls the swinger down. Objects move when the forces acting on them are unbalanced. In the time that follows your swing experiment, use the terms "**push**" and "**pull**" as often as possible within the context of everyday activities. Here are some examples:

- The cook is bringing our milk and breakfast fruit. How does she make the cart move?

- There is a lot of noise in the parking lot. Let's **pull** the window shut.

- It's hard to get your arm in your jacket sleeve. Can you **push** your hand through?

Remember to ask children to explain their understandings to one another. They can also ask the school staff, "Is it hard to push the cart?" or, "Can I help you pull?"

Elaborate

Take a walking field trip around the building to find something that can move by a push or a pull. In a school, it might be a cart of library books, office supplies, or custodial materials. In a home environment, it might be a wagon full of toys. Then find a way to change the mass of the moving object. Add more books, supplies, or materials to the cart, or add more toys to the wagon. Ask students to measure and compare how hard it is to move the bigger load. (This is a great opportunity to involve other adults in your science experiences.)

A wheel is a simple machine that makes pushing or pulling easier. Continue the walking tour to find all the wheels that are used in the school. Do the wheels have brakes or clamps to stop them? Children may also observe which wheels are smooth and which are bumpy or treaded. Later you can connect those observations to experiences with friction.

Reading the book *Newton and Me* (see below) can encourage children to imagine themselves as scientists. Try it under a tree! But be careful not to get into too much detail about gravity. That comes in the next unit, as another force that can be sensed.

Evaluate

Take a picture of a child on playground equipment. (Ideally, have the teacher take a picture or give the children a drawing.) Then ask children to draw arrows to show the forces they can sense. (Remember, these are not all the possible forces—only those that children can feel.) Then let children bring their photos home to discuss with their families.

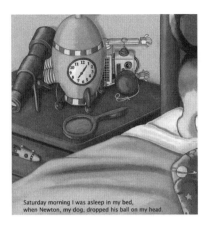

Saturday morning I was asleep in my bed,
when Newton, my dog, dropped his ball on my head.

Push Power

by Janet Wong

I pull with my hands.
My wagon is stuck.
I push harder with legs.
This time I'm in luck.
My wagon gets out
of the mud
but—
wait!

It zooms
down the hill
straight into the lake!

Integrate

Lynne Mayer's NSTA/CBC Outstanding Science Trade Book *Newton and Me* includes many authentic experiences about force and motion for the youngest learners. Each colorful page invites discussion of real-world examples. The book is ideal for an introductory literature experience. You can also use it to review ideas throughout a unit on force and motion. The publisher (Arbordale Publishing) has a corresponding website with additional activities.

Use the various toys shown in the book (such as the wagon) to have children illustrate pushes and pulls. Reading the book a second time, children can identify things that make objects harder to move (weight in a wagon) and things that make objects easier to move (wheels).

The story of Newton (page 39) helps children imagine themselves as observant scientists. For younger children, consider peer partnerships in which an older child reads the prompts and then records the younger child's dictated responses. Spend a bit of time on the question "Could things fall up?" That is the bridge to unit 2.

The poem on this page, "Push Power" by Janet Wong, is a rhythmic way to emphasize the concepts in this unit.

More Literature to Integrate

- *Move It! Motion, Forces, and You* by Adrienne Mason includes many activities for children and families, including "Push It," an activity that compares the force needed to push heavy and light things.

- *Thud! Wile E. Coyote Experiments with Forces and Motion* by Mark Weakland provides humorous but accurate cartoon illustrations and experiments about force and motion that children can enjoy both reading and doing. You can find more details about this book in unit 5 (page 76), where we discuss friction.

Engineering Challenge

Safety engineers design and communicate ideas to make machines safer for people to use. The swing, slide, or other equipment on a child care program's playground will usually be inspected for safety at regular intervals. (This is almost always done by the program's insurer.)

Take children on a tour of the playground again, looking for safety features on the equipment. These might include soft surfaces under the swing and slide, ridges on the slide, distance between equipment, and so on. Photograph the swings and use the photos to make safety posters or video messages. For the youngest engineers, provide a word wall with choices for caution words.

Content Background

While pushes and pulls are familiar forces, children may have significant misconceptions about these forces. For nearly two thousand years (since the time of the Greek scholar Aristotle), most people thought that a force was needed to keep something moving. It is an idea that comes from observation. You push a cart, and after you stop pushing, it slows down. It wasn't until English scientist Isaac Newton came along in the 1600s CE that scientists began to look at motion in an analytical way. Newton studied mass (how much matter), force (push or pull), and momentum (a measure of velocity and matter in motion).

A push starts a cart moving. The forces of friction and air resistance stop it. The forces don't "run out." It's the same basic process when things drop. Gravity pulls an object down. The floor or table pushes the object up. If the forces acting on an object are balanced, the object doesn't move. If the forces are unbalanced, the object moves.

As with all the physical science phenomena we observe, the movement of a child on a swing is far more complicated than it seems. It involves more than just a push and a pull. Of course, gravity does pull down as the swing pushes up. But the direction of motion is actually angular. There is torque at the top of the swing's ropes or chains, as well as friction from the connection there and from the air. Pumping of the swinger's legs creates another set of forces. None of these forces needs to be analyzed in this lesson.

 EARLY EXPLORERS

The images in *Newton and Me* show many ways to use a wagon or cart to experience pushes and pulls. As you share the story, have a wagon or cart handy. Blocks or books can become the load as children follow Newton and his boy through the story. The book also features many other common toys, including balls, that you can use during reading. Put some in a big drawer that you **pull** to begin science play and **push** to help clean up. Arbordale Publishing's website offers a video to help young children and their guides.

Sample Common Core Standards

Describe the connection between a series of historical events, scientific ideas or concepts, or steps in technical procedures in a text. (CCSS.ELA-Literacy.RI.2.3) (CCSS Initiative 2016a, 13)

Directly compare two objects with a measurable attribute in common, to see which object has "more of"/"less of" the attribute, and describe the difference. (CCSS.Math.Content.K.MD.A.2) (CCSS Initiative 2016b, 12)

A playground swing is essentially a pendulum. The period of the pendulum (how fast it moves back and forth) is related to the length of the rope or chain, not to the mass of the bob, or passenger. No matter how hard you push at the beginning, most swingers will settle into the same period after a short time unless they use their muscles to create more force. When swingers pump their legs, the energy of their muscles creates forward momentum and adds to the original push. (It's a bit like ice skaters pulling in their arms to speed up.) The push doesn't run out. Rather, it is opposed by other forces. The forces that slow down a swinger are pulls, like friction from the rope or chain, wind resistance, and gravity.

Young children won't realize all the forces involved and will not be able to think about all the possible variables that are involved as they swing. But the swing experience has other lessons that are appropriate building blocks at this age level. Just beginning to think about pushes and pulls is a great first step on a path toward understanding. Asking children to discuss their swing experiences enhances their understanding. The idea of developing a fair test challenges children to think about all the things that might make a test unfair. Later on in their scientific careers, children will understand that these things are called variables.

Be an Engineer!

Engineers design things. They also explain things.

When you buy something, you get directions that tell you how to use it.

An engineer wrote the directions.

Can you be an engineer? Explain how to be safe on your playground.

Make a poster to help children use the playground safely.

You can draw a picture or take a photo.

Use science words on your poster.

Here are some ideas you could use:

Don't _____ too hard.

When you push someone, make sure that _____ .

Look under your swing. The ground should be _____ .

Don't _____the slide.

Try It!

You can **push** or **pull** a cart.

A spring scale measures a pull.

When you attach a spring scale to a cart, you can measure how much pull it takes to move the cart.

Look at the numbers on the spring scale. Can you count them aloud?

Hook the spring scale to a cart.

How much pull do you need to move it?

_____

Put one book on the cart. How much pull?

_____

Now put two books on the cart. How much pull?

_____

Predict: How much pull will you need for three books?

_____

Now test your prediction.

Was your prediction right?

_____

Isaac Newton: STEM Star

Have you ever sat under a tree? Did something fall?

Long ago, a scientist named Isaac Newton sat under a tree. He saw things fall. He wondered why.

Once an apple fell near Isaac. He wondered, "Why did the apple fall down from the tree? Could anything fall up?"

Gravity is the pull we feel from Earth. It makes things fall.

Newton continued to wonder. He found answers by doing experiments. He talked about gravity. He wrote three rules that describe motion of all objects.

Scientists today continue to use Isaac Newton's rules to predict how pushes and pulls work.

Have you ever sat under a tree and wondered? What did you want to know? _____

_____

Pretend you are sitting under a tree. Tell a story of what you see around you. What do you hear? What do you feel? What do you smell? _____

_____

_____

What is falling from the tree? _____

_____

Dear Families:

To begin our study of physical science, we are studying pushes and pulls. These are common experiences for children everywhere they go. You can help support our science investigations by using appropriate language as you provide company for your children.

A force is a **push** or a **pull**. It changes the movement of an object—sometimes speeding it up or slowing it down, sometimes changing the direction of its movement, sometimes changing its position. An object in motion remains in motion until forces like friction slow it down.

Almost every time you enter a door of a commercial building, there will be a sign saying "Push" or "Pull." Read these signs as you demonstrate their meaning to your child. While you are at home, ask your child to help you push or pull. The grocery cart, the lawn mower, and the vacuum cleaner can all be tools for learning. We are using a spring scale to measure pulls.

Pushes and pulls are especially important in sports. We push a bat or a soccer ball. We pull when we wrestle or play tug-of-war. We are also marking the pushes and pulls we feel on photos of children as they play. When we use science words to reinforce these ideas at home, it makes learning a lot more fun.

Many of our science lessons integrate science with technology, engineering, and mathematics. You might be familiar with the acronym STEM, which stands for <u>s</u>cience, <u>t</u>echnology, <u>e</u>ngineering, and <u>m</u>ath. STEM is not a separate subject, but a way of thinking. STEM learning emphasizes problem solving and innovation. Your children may take the ideas from our lessons and apply them to questions that they invent themselves. "How hard do I have to push to make a big box move?" "What happens when I pull on the chain for this ceiling light?" When the experience is safe, encourage your children to try! And in the conversation that follows, make sure that you leave room for ideas that include measurement and invention.

Thanks for being great STEM partners. And have fun.

Falling Down

UNIT 2

The Big Question: What Happens When Objects Do Not Have Something to Hold Them Up?

Creating Context

In unit 1, we included a reading about Isaac Newton. According to legend, his investigations into motion began when he observed apples falling from a tree. We asked if things could fall up. Now we explore the answer.

From the perspective of someone on this planet, everything falls down until a **force** pushes it up. The earth pulls the object, and the object pulls the earth, but the difference between the force of pull exerted by the object and by the earth is so great that we only sense the pull of the planet. Objects move when forces are unbalanced. We see the effect of unbalanced forces when something falls, but we seldom think of the balanced forces that keep it from falling further.

Engage

Begin by dropping objects. Pretend to accidentally drop something that makes an interesting plop (like a beanbag or a figure made of cookie dough or clay). Then integrate a book. Explore how different things fall with Vicki Cobb's book *I Fall Down*. Her text models good dialogue. Read the first part of the book aloud, and use open dialogue like that in the text as you repeat some of the investigations. Remember to emphasize that things **fall down.**

Solids, liquids, and balloons filled with gas undergo interesting changes when they hit a surface, which is an opposing **force**. For each investigation, ask children, "How does it **fall**?" It **falls down**!

by Vicki Cobb illustrated by Julia Gorton

Sample Next Generation Science Standards

Disciplinary Core Ideas

PS2.A: Forces and Motion

- Pushes and pulls can have different strengths and directions. (K-PS2-1, K-PS2-2)
- Pushing or pulling on an object can change the speed or direction of its motion and can start or stop it. (K-PS2-1, K-PS2-2)

Performance Expectation

Students who demonstrate understanding can:

Analyze data to determine if a design solution works as intended to change the speed or direction of an object with a push or a pull. (K-PS2-2)

(NGSS Lead States 2013)

Safety Note

Don't drop things that might shatter. Remember, little scientists will want to look closely and will need eye protection. If you drop things from a greater height, the risk is higher. Children are naturally curious, so expect them to get closer than they should.

Don't let children stand on chairs to drop objects. A stair or riser can make a safer perch.

In this unit's engineering challenge, you could empty the eggs to avoid a mess. But a mess may be half the fun!

Explore

In the middle of her book *I Fall Down*, Cobb explores "dropping races." Share the activity with children. Allow them to compare any two objects that won't break or shatter.

Then reintroduce the idea of a fair test. Ask children to find two objects about the same size and shape. If your program has a set of risers or a safely railed stairwell, you can increase the distance that the objects fall in the children's dropping races. The children at the bottom of the drop should be far away from the landing zone, for safety. Don't forget to ask children to predict what will happen before they do the test.

Explain

Earth pulls on all objects. We call the pull of an object (such as a planet) on any other object gravity. If something (such as a table or the floor) pushes up on an object, it doesn't fall. But if nothing is pushing up on the object, it **falls down**. When an astronaut gets far from the earth, the pull of our planet's gravity gets weaker. But things are always pulling and pushing one another.

Ask children to explain to one another why things don't fall up, or why they stop falling when another force pushes up. If you have access to pictures of interesting things falling (such as rocks, leaves, or toys), these can also be good discussion prompts.

Elaborate

Parachutes help slow down things that fall. So do spider webs, maple samaras, and helicopter rotors. This idea will be explored in more depth on page 107 of unit 8, when children explore how air affects movement. Look for things that help slow down falling objects in videos, in photos, and in the environment. Ask children to catch a soft object that falls down (such as a beanbag). As children catch, they should say, "I push up."

In preparation for this unit's engineering challenge, ask families to take their children on a trip to a grocery or gift store to see how packaging can prevent damage to things that fall.

A variation on the engineering challenge might involve comparing cookie packaging. Bring a variety of packaged cookies, still in their packaging, to your program's cafeteria or lunch table. Allow children to drop the packages onto the table to see which package works best for protecting its contents. In a dining setting, of course, the broken pieces taste just as good as the whole cookies. (See note in the introduction, on page 28 under "Classroom Management and Safety," on not eating in a science lab setting.)

Evaluate

The classic Rube Goldberg cartoon machine shows a series of pushes and pulls. (See link in appendix D.) Goldberg cartoons show how falling might be used to make a series of actions happen. Choose a Goldberg cartoon and enlarge the image. Find the places in the cartoon where things fall down. A similar set of actions exists in the game Mousetrap. (This vintage game is back in production, and old editions are often available at resale shops or garage sales.) For each place where something falls, is pushed, or is pulled in the diagram or the game, ask children to point and use the appropriate term or to add arrows.

Integrate

I Fall Down by Vicki Cobb includes a number of other simple experiments to emulate while modeling very open classroom dialogue.

 EARLY EXPLORERS

Some things that fall down come up again. They bounce. Young children can look for things that bounce. Collect pairs of balls that are about the same size but made of different materials, such as a Ping-Pong ball, a ball from a jacks set, and a heavier small ball. Ask for a prediction: "Will it bounce?" Then try dropping each ball.

Familiar children's songs include the motion of falling down. "Ring around the Rosie" has this physical action. So does "Itsy Bitsy Spider." These songs are great ways to reinforce vocabulary.

 TEACHER TIP

With every drop, at least two forces are acting: the force of gravity pulling down and the force of whatever stops the object pushing up. While that idea may not come naturally to young observers, you can build a foundation for the idea by asking, "What stopped the drop? Could it drop forever?"

Of course, there is also wind resistance. That's really why some things fall slower or faster than others on Earth. That idea will come much later in your explorers' scientific careers. But you can explore it in a qualitative way by comparing objects about the same size and shape and objects of different forms.

More Literature to Integrate

- The book *Motion: Push and Pull, Fast and Slow* by Darlene Stille offers great examples and easy classroom experiments. Stille suggests that you ask children to invent a dance with pushes and pulls. You can use the song "All Fall Down" on page 46 to get your scientists moving.

- *Push and Pull* by Patricia J. Murphy is an ideal book to read to the group, then hand to individual readers.

- *Egg Drop* by Mini Grey can provide context for the engineering challenge.

Content Background

All matter has the capacity of attracting—pulling on—all other matter. This **force** acts on matter in proportion to its mass. The physical term is "gravitation," or "gravity." Gravity doesn't just move objects; it accelerates them. As objects **fall**, they go faster and faster. The acceleration of gravity near the surface of the earth is 9.8 meters per second per second (m/s/s). But that theoretical rate applies only to an object in free fall, without air or other forces acting on it. That's not something a child or anyone else is likely to observe.

Gravitation is directly related to the mass of an object. A physicist would explain that mass has resistance to change in motion or inertia. That's why it takes a force to speed up an object or to slow it down. It also takes a force to change the direction of a moving object.

Another way to think of mass is that it's the amount of matter in an object. It is reflected in its inertia. Mass is related to the number and kind of particles per unit of space. Most of any object is empty space, but some materials (such as lead) have more particles per unit of space than others. This is a measure of density.

Weight is the effect of a planet's gravitation on an object's mass. If we took an object to the moon, its mass would be the same, but its weight would change. A spring scale or bathroom scale measures weight. A pan balance measures mass. Objects would fall on the moon or any planet. Even an object out in space is subject to small pulls from masses around it. (If an object was exactly halfway between Earth and the moon, it would be pulled toward Earth because Earth is more massive than the moon.)

We often think of the force of gravity pulling **down**, but if an object isn't falling, the surface it is on (or the thing holding it up) is exerting an equal but opposite force. The idea of balanced and unbalanced forces will be difficult for young children, but we can begin to introduce authentic experiences as they grow. We often think there is no gravity in a space shuttle or space station. But that's not true. Physicists call it "microgravity" because it is so much less than what we observe on our planet.

Vicki Cobb's idea of a dropping race is complicated by the size, shape, and mass of the objects we drop. The acceleration of Earth's gravity is the same on every object we drop. But air resistance affects the speed of the racers. If those objects were in a total vacuum, they would all fall at the same speed.

Engineering Challenge

Engineers design packages so that things do not break when they fall down. An egg carton is a package designed to protect eggs. For this activity, you may choose to use whole eggs or ones that have been emptied through small holes at either end. Provide simple materials that could be used to package the eggs. Set a size and weight for a fair test.

Tell the children, "Imagine you have to design a package to send eggs to a friend. Use some of these materials to make a safe package":

- paper
- cloth
- Styrofoam
- bubble wrap
- Easter grass
- starch packing peanuts
- paper cups
- cardboard

- wood chips
- tape
- paper towels
- balloons

Tell the children, "Our test must be fair. So I will tell you how big and heavy your package can be."

Sing the following words to the tune of "Ring around the Rosie." At the end of the song, children "all fall down."

All Fall Down

Walking through the neighborhood,

running through our own town,

all because of gravity,

we all fall down!

Dear Families:

We are studying more physical science. This unit's topic is gravity! We are exploring how things fall. Of course, they always **fall down**.

Things fall all the time all around us. Most of the time, we don't want that to happen! But you can experiment with falling by dropping soft things such as pillows and toys or safe things such as clay or soap onto a table or floor. You can also ask children to observe the shape of something that falls, such as a lump of pizza dough. A force pushing up (from the table or floor) stops the dough from falling and changes its shape, too.

The falling that we observe is the result of what we call gravity. In fact, every bit of matter attracts every other bit of matter. But a planet pulls far harder than anything on it. So our lessons have focused on the pull of Earth. Our vocabulary words for the week are "**force**," "**fall**,"and "**down**." Can something fall up? Not on a planet. But it's fun to think about how things can act when gravity is very low. We'll be watching a video from NASA called *Toys in Space*, showing how common toys can work in a place where there is very little gravity. You can find it on YouTube if you search "toys in space."

For our engineering challenge, we are going to experiment with packaging that might prevent an egg from breaking when it falls. You can help your child prepare for this activity by taking a walk through the grocery store. Look for packages that protect cookies and eggs. Or in a gift store, ask the clerk to explain how things that could break easily are protected when they go home.

Thanks for being great STEM partners. And have fun.

Try It!

Find things of similar size and shape that cannot break easily. Predict which will fall first. Then try it!

Dropping Races

Predict! Draw what you think will happen.			
Tennis ball vs. softball	Domino vs. alphabet block	Yarn ball vs. crumpled paper	Key vs. washers
Observe! Draw what happened.			

Galileo Galilei: STEM Star

Galileo was a scientist. He was an engineer, too.

He lived four hundred years ago in Italy.

He was curious about just about everything!

In church, he wondered why the lamps swung back and forth.

He wondered about planets farther away than the ones he could see.

When something fell, he wondered why it went down and not up.

Some people say that Galileo held dropping races from a tower near his home.

Imagine that you could talk to Galileo. You want to ask a question:

"What happens when heavy and light things fall at the same time?"

What would he say?

Heavy and Light

The Big Question: Which Objects Are Heavy? Which Are Light?

Creating Context

There are different kinds of matter. Matter can be described and classified by observable properties. We can see or feel some properties with our senses. Weight is one of those properties that we can sense. We use terms like "**heavy**" and "**light**"to describe the property of weight. Heavy objects need more push or pull to change their motion than light objects need.

Engage

Ask a volunteer to come to the front of the room and stand with eyes shut and hands extended. Give the volunteer two deli containers of the same size with different-colored lids, each filled with objects of different weights. Ask the volunteer to tell which container is heavy and which is light.

Then repeat the activity with different objects. This time, let the children (but not the volunteer) see the objects. Ask the children to predict which container the volunteer will say is heavy. Have the children vote silently by raising their hands.

Explore

Organize the children into two groups. Give each group two same-size deli containers. Ask each group to put something heavy in one container and something light in the other container. The groups can then trade containers. The members of each group close their eyes and try to tell which container is heavy and which is light. (The size of the containers

 TEACHER TIP

When two objects of the same size have different weights, that's because they have different densities. Density is a concept that young children won't fully understand for many years. But you can use physical models and examples to help young children take the first steps toward understanding. For example, you can fill up the holes in a sponge with water to make the sponge heavier. Children might use their own terms, such as "thicker" or "fuller," to describe what they imagine. That's a good beginning.

Allow children to carry two different backpacks or cloth bags, one containing something heavy and the other containing something light, and pantomime how they feel as they walk. You can share pictures of pack animals (such as llamas, burros, and elephants) to encourage conversation about heavy loads. Also, many children's books feature people or animals carrying heavy things. When you're reading such a book, stop to ask, "Do you think it was heavy?"

limits the size of the items, but using same-size containers encourages children to make a fair comparison.)

After the activity, set up two areas in the classroom—one for the heavy objects and one for the light ones. Discuss with the children whether the heavy objects have something in common and whether the light ones also have something in common. For example, there may be more metal objects in the heavy collection, and more paper or plastic in the light collection.

Explain

Every substance has properties. We use the words "**heavy**" and "**light**" to describe the property of weight. Weight is different from size. A big object, such as a pillow, might have less weight than a small object, such as a rock. Weight is really the pull of the earth on an object. Weight is a sign of how much mass the object contains. When an astronaut travels from Earth to the moon, the astronaut is the same person in both places and has the same mass. But the astronaut has different weights on the earth and moon. The moon is smaller, so its gravitational pull on the astronaut is weaker, and the astronaut weighs less on the moon. Ask children to explain to one another why it is harder to lift some objects than others.

Elaborate

To build beginning ideas about how much matter is in an object, give children two sponges of the same size and shape. Compare the sponges. Then wet one of the sponges. Ask children to explain why they think a wet sponge is heavier than a dry sponge. (A reasonable explanation that's developmentally appropriate at this age is that the holes are filled with water, so there is less empty space—but any consistent explanation is appropriate.) This introductory experience can build understanding about density as the learner matures.

Evaluate

Build a balance. (To help children understand, compare a balance to a seesaw.) Put an object on one side and challenge a child to find an object that is heavier to put on the other side. Note: You can also use the clothes hanger balance shown in unit 8 (page 106) for this activity if the objects you want to compare have small areas that can be clipped by clothespins.

Ask the children to look again at the heavy and light items they've collected. Introduce a new object and ask a child to decide if it should go in the heavy group or the light group. The child can do this using senses or using a balance.

Following is a sample of a formative assessment, or probe, by Page Keeley designed for early childhood. Keeley's probes are research-based tools targeted at the sorts of misconceptions we know children have at this age. The probes also encourage development of language arts skills such as argumentation.

In this case, the probe is designed to assess whether a child understands conservation of mass. This was a key schema or logical structure that Jean Piaget studied seventy-five years ago. Appendix D can direct you to video of a dialogue with young children about conservation of mass.

TEACHER TIP

Many building materials are also great classroom tools. Hardware stores offer flat plastic strips that you can make into balances. You can use triangular doorstops as fulcrums.

Snap Blocks

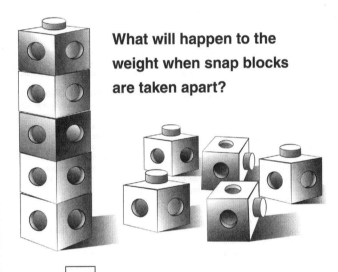

What will happen to the weight when snap blocks are taken apart?

☐ They will weigh **more.**

☐ They will weigh **less.**

☐ They will weigh the **same.**

What are you thinking?

Reprinted with permission from Keeley, P., "Snap Blocks" in *Uncovering Student Ideas in Primary Science*. Arlington, VA: National Science Teachers Association, 2013, p. 59.

Sample Next Generation Science Standards

Disciplinary Core Idea

PS1.A: Structure and Properties of Matter

Matter can be described and classified by its observable properties. (2-PS1-1)

Performance Expectation

Students who demonstrate understanding can:

Plan and conduct an investigation to compare the effects of different strengths or different directions of pushes and pulls on the motion of an object. (K-PS2-1)

(NGSS Lead States 2013)

Sample Common Core Standards

Describe the connection between a series of historical events, scientific ideas or concepts, or steps in technical procedures in a text. (CCSS.ELA-Literacy.RI.2.3) (CCSS Initiative 2016a, 13)

Directly compare two objects with a measurable attribute in common, to see which object has "more of"/"less of" the attribute, and describe the difference. (CCSS.Math.Content.K.MD.A.2) (CCSS Initiative 2016b, 12)

Integrate

While young children won't have a deep understanding of how gravity changes on different bodies in our solar system, almost all of them have the sense that things are lighter on the moon. Show students the classic footage of astronauts on the moon at www.nasa.gov/mission_pages/apollo/40th /apollo11_tapes.html, and tell them to imagine they are lighter. Ask them to create their own "moonwalk," imitating the astronauts.

What could the children do in a place where things are lighter? Could they throw farther? Jump higher?

Read aloud the award-winning book *Eight Days Gone* by Linda McReynolds. Ask children to shut their eyes and imagine they are astronauts.

NASA's website offers videos of the project International Toys in Space, which you can use with children. (See www.nasa.gov/audience/foreducators/microgravity/home/toys-in-space.html.) In space, these objects appear to be free of gravity. Of course, there is a tiny gravitational pull from many masses around them, but that won't be visible to children. Play with the toys in the classroom, then watch the astronauts play with the same toys in space.

More Literature to Integrate

- *Move It! Motion, Forces, and You* by Adrienne Mason offers many activities, including a variation of the plastic container experiment in this unit. Mason suggests filling the containers with pasta and rocks, and asking children to predict which will take more force to slide.

- *Awesome Experiments in Force and Motion* by Michael A. DiSpezio includes more good experiments, some appropriate for older or more advanced students.

- Trevor Lai's *Tomo Explores the World* is a story about a child of a fishing family who has a great imagination. It is a great way to spark young imaginations.

Engineering Challenge

A standard fishing pole must have something heavy, a sinker, and something light, a bobber. Together, the sinker and the bobber keep the hook down in the water, but not too deep. Give each child a pole and a string. Instead of a fishhook, use a small plastic hook like the kind that displays socks and other products in stores.

 **TEACHER TIP**

We often see images of astronauts in the International Space Station or in a spacecraft and use the term "weightless." But, of course, no place exists where gravitation doesn't affect mass. Scientists use the term "microgravity" instead. You can accurately say "much less weight" to describe microgravity, because objects in space are farther from the pull of Earth or another planet, moon, or mass.

Because young children have so much exposure to phenomena that are far away in time or space (like imaginary walks on the moon), they often seem to have sophisticated knowledge of these situations. Their understanding about gravity and falling may, however, be confused by cartoons and computer games. That's why for young children, it is important to stick to the physical phenomena that they can actually sense. Emphasize Earth's gravity and the idea that things fall down when they don't have forces holding them up.

Sample Common Core Standards

Describe familiar people, places, things, and events and, with prompting and support, provide additional detail. (CCSS.ELA-Literacy.SL.K.4) (CCSS Initiative 2016a, 23)

Describe measurable attributes of objects, such as length or weight. Describe several measurable attributes of a single object. (CCSS.Math.Content.K.MD.A.1) (CCSS Initiative 2016b, 12)

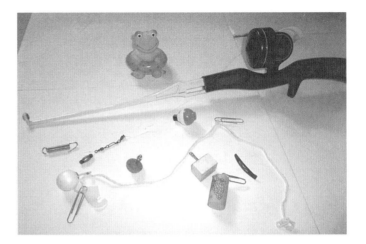

Provide a collection of small objects that can be attached easily to the string. Create loops in the string for easy attachment of the objects, and put paper clips on the objects so that small hands can clip them easily to the string.

Objects that attach easily include key fobs, big paper clips, Styrofoam packing peanuts, Ping-Pong balls, and inexpensive jewelry. For added fun, use an aquarium of water and a toy fish. If an aquarium is not easily available, use a big sink or bucket.

Content Background

Mass is the amount of matter in an object. To a physicist, it is the inertial property of the substance or its resistance to a change in motion. Weight is the result of gravitation acting on that mass.

But at the early childhood level, only weight is relevant. It is a property of a substance that can be felt with the senses and that is related to the idea of a pull. Using the practices of science, children can ask questions and define problems, plan and carry out investigations, collect data from their senses, and argue from their own evidence about weight.

Density is the mass per unit of volume. It is a derived measurement, and truly understanding it won't come until middle school or secondary school. But a more descriptive understanding of density—the "degree of compactness" of a substance—can be experiential and intuitive. Comparing dry and wet sponges (in this lesson) is just one way that children can physically experience density. Comparing similar-size samples of matter (like rubber versus Nerf balls or wood versus plastic blocks) can be framed in the context of a fair test.

The fishing pole activity in this unit exploits another property, buoyancy. The ability of an object to float depends both on its weight and the amount of water (or another liquid) that is displaced. So if a heavy object is very compact, it will displace (push away) a smaller amount of water than an object that is the same weight but wider and flatter, which displaces more water.

Dear Families:

This week we are learning about weight, which is a property of matter. We are classifying objects as **heavy** and **light** . You can help by extending this experience at home and practicing our new vocabulary at home and in the community. Pick one safe object in the kitchen and ask your child to feel it, then to find something heavier. Gravity is a force that pulls things toward the earth. The children are experimenting with pairs of objects of similar size and shape but different weights. We describe these objects as **heavy** or **light** . We test for these properties with our senses.

If you have a home bathroom scale, ask your child to stand on it, note your child's weight, and then find something (like a pile of books) that is about the same weight. Or while you're cooking, use a small food scale to find something that is almost as heavy as another small object, such as a salt shaker. You can also ask your child to weigh small boxes or cans on a food scale. Your child might help you group heavy things to put on low shelves and lighter things to put on higher shelves.

For a group activity, we will need many small, clean plastic food containers (such as those that contain deli foods). We'd appreciate extra containers if you have them. We'll be filling them with different objects that are **heavier** or **lighter**. You can do the same at home. Fill the containers, then ask your child to compare the weights of the containers. Challenge your child to put a relatively light object in one container and fill the other container with something heavier.

In our engineering challenge, we are building a fishing line with a bobber (a plastic float) and a sinker (something heavy to make the fishing lure sink). If you have the opportunity to go fishing with your child or watch a movie about fishing, please share it with us!

Thanks for being great STEM partners. Have fun.

Try It!

Put heavy things in a box marked *H*.

Put light things in a box marked *L*.

Trade boxes with a friend.

Then draw what's inside each box.

What's in the heavy box?

What's in the light box?

Be an Engineer!

When you go fishing, you want a hook to go down just far enough in the water to attract the right fish, but not too far! A fisher puts a heavy weight near the hook so it will go down. That's called a sinker.

Then the fisher puts a lighter thing that floats, a bobber, higher on the string. You want just the right amount of string to reach the fish. The bobber holds up the hook so it doesn't drop too deep in the water.

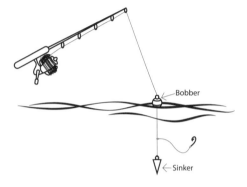

Design your own fishing pole. Find a light thing that will float for a bobber and a heavy thing that will pull the hook down for a sinker. Then test your fishing pole in water.

Draw a picture of what you have built.

Juliana Berners and Charles Kirby: STEM Stars

Cats and bears love fish.

So do people.

The first people probably knew how to catch fish to eat.

They used short sticks, spears, nets, or even their hands!

An *angle* is a pole. People who fish are called *anglers*.

Juliana Berners lived in England five hundred years ago. She wrote a book with a very odd name: *The Treatyse of Fysshynge wyth an Angle*.

That means "a story about fishing with a pole"! This story helped people catch fish better.

Charles Kirby lived in England four hundred years ago. He invented the bent fishhook that lots of people use.

Why do you think a hook is good for fishing? _____

_____

_____

What other invention could help people catch more fish? _____

_____

_____

Rolling, Rolling, Rolling

The Big Question: When Gravity Starts an Object in Motion, What Makes It Stop?

Creating Context

Gravity is a force, a pull from the earth that can start an object in motion. Other forces can stop an object that's falling. Friction is one force that can slow an object down. Both surface contacts and air can cause friction, but it is easiest for children to observe, measure, and manipulate the friction between sliding surfaces.

Children will not fully understand these forces until later in their scientific careers. But they can begin by describing the effects of forces they can sense. Becoming aware of forces builds confidence and capacity.

Engage

On your program's handicap ramp (or on any ramp), **roll** a variety of balls (soccer, baseball, golf). If going outside isn't practical, show children an image or video of a large ball or snowball rolling down a hill. Ask, "What started it? What could stop it?"

Ask children to tell a story to a partner that begins, "Once I was standing at the bottom of a hill and looked up. I saw a giant ball rolling toward me." Encourage children to tell their partners what happened next.

Safety Note

When we set up ramp experiments, we often move into a large open space. A ball or car may travel very far after leaving the ramp! It is a tripping hazard—especially for the adults who may be using the area. Warn the rest of your community and, if necessary, put up signs: "Caution: scientists at work!"

Sample Next Generation Science Standards

Disciplinary Core Ideas

PS2.A: Forces and Motion

- Pushes and pulls can have different strengths and directions. (K-PS2-1, K-PS2-2)
- Pushing or pulling on an object can change the speed or direction of its motion and can start or stop it. (K-PS2-1, K-PS2-2)

Performance Expectation

Students who demonstrate understanding can:

Plan and conduct an investigation to compare the effects of different strengths or different directions of pushes and pulls on the motion of an object. (K-PS2-1)

(NGSS Lead States 2013)

Explore

Set up a ramp in a hallway or some other open area. (L-shaped molding from a hardware store makes an ideal ramp for small balls. You could also use flat ramps that are part of toy car sets.) Provide a group of objects (mostly round, but some not so round) that can be rolled down the ramp and compared.

Prepare markers that can be used to record the distance each object rolls. (Suction cups into which pencils with paper flags have been embedded work well. You can also use globs of clay to mount the flags. Sticky notes can serve, but sometimes move in the hustle of a class activity.) Children can measure the distance the objects **roll** in feet, yards, or giant steps. Any consistent measuring unit serves well. For the youngest students, use paper rulers end to end, and don't worry about fractions of units.

Then create a graph. Stretch out lengths of wide holiday ribbon from the end of the ramp to the end of the run and cut them where the cars stop. Mount the ribbons on the classroom or hallway wall. Now you have a bar graph for each child's experiment. This is a way for young scientists to begin the transition from physical measurements to representational diagrams.

Explain

Forces can start or stop something moving. They can also change the direction that something moves. The movement of a ball or marble down a ramp is pulled by the force of gravity. The pull doesn't run out. The force of friction (a little from the air, a lot from the surface) opposes the pull of gravity. Children won't understand this fully for a long time, but using consistent language can build a foundation for future learning.

Elaborate

Repeat the experiment, and ask children to use their own air force (breath blown through a straw) to try to change the direction of the ball after it leaves the ramp. This experience can help prepare children for later investigations (unit 8, page 105) of the properties of gases (the type of matter we call air).

Remember to ask children to **predict** what will happen whenever you introduce a new variable. Predictions can be words, pictures, or numbers.

Evaluate

Ask children to classify new objects as to whether they will **roll** or not roll. Ask them to **predict** which will roll faster.

Take a photograph of the children's data (graph or chart). Ask children to explain the experiment and the result. The website www.fotobabble.com provides a very easy way to add sound to a photograph.

Integrate

Read sections of Adrienne Mason's book *Move It!* that emphasize explanations, like "Puffing Power." Follow the directions, allowing children to discuss how to make this a fair test and to discuss and develop their own ways of measuring the results. Note that there will be more activities using air power in unit 8.

 TEACHER TIP

Watch the video on modeling at the early childhood level from Peep and the Big Wide World at http://peepandthe bigwideworld.com/en/educators /teaching-strategies/1/family- child-care-educators/2/learning- environments/17/ramps/. This video shows an open-ended experience with ramps and rolling.

EARLY EXPLORERS

Classification skills are important for early engineers. Set up a large ramp in one corner of the room. Allow children to send any safe, unbreakable object down the ramp. Put objects that roll in one place or container and those that don't in another place or container. Add new objects to the classification activity over time. As you share stories with the children, ask them to identify objects in the illustrations that roll.

More Literature to Integrate

- *And Everyone Shouted, "Pull!"* by Claire Llewellyn provides a first look at force and motion for young children.

- *Motion: Push and Pull, Fast and Slow* by Darlene Stille offers great examples and easy classroom experiments, including activities with paper and balls to compare falling rates.

Engineering Challenge

When children begin to **roll** things, they naturally think of toy cars. The same experiment can be done with balls, but cars will go farther and faster than most objects. To create a fair test, children can compare two toy cars of similar structure and make one of them heavier by taping coins or metal nuts on top of it.

Look at this unit's content background for a bit of science, but don't get too involved in explaining why one car is faster than another. The point of activities like this is to explore how we **predict**, measure, and use data to discuss or argue. The forces that vary in toy cars are often inside the wheel and axle. Teaching children to ask a question, design a fair test, and look at the results is a great goal in itself.

Content Background

One of the most persistent misconceptions about motion is that once an object is in motion, the motion eventually "runs out." In fact, an object in motion stays in motion, and an object at rest remains at rest, until another force acts on it. The reason we appear to observe motion "running out" is that the moving object is being slowed by another force. That's usually friction.

There are four kinds of friction: static, sliding, rolling, and fluid. Static friction holds an object in place (imagine a wood block on a slightly sloped wooden ramp). With sliding friction, the force is weaker. The object can move, like a child on a slide, but a force slows it down. Rolling friction is even weaker. A car or machine wheel lined with ball bearings would be an example. And fluid friction is the resistance of air or a liquid like water. Watch a feather fall slowly and you'll understand.

When students experiment with balls and ramps, the rolling friction on the ramp or surface eventually slows down the object. But most small balls can go very far. With cars on ramps, the friction within the toy's axles is a major factor. Children won't see that, but they might observe that heavier cars slow down more quickly. That's really not due to their weight, but because the axles have more friction inside.

Like all experiments in force and motion at this age, the most important goal is to emphasize that our senses can provide good observations that can be recorded, measured, and used to answer questions.

 TEACHER TIP

The movement of a toy car is often controlled more by friction within the car's wheels than friction between the car and the ramp. In general, a heavier car will have more grip on the ramp and not slip as much. It may also slow down more quickly because of internal friction. But remember, the point of the activity is to measure, observe, and share ideas.

Rolling Balls

There are many ways to measure the distance a ball rolls after it leaves a ramp.

Children can use wide ribbons, then hang them at the front of the room to compare.

They can also use rulers, meter sticks, or trundle wheels, depending on what's available. This sample graph is numbered 1 to 10, but you can use any number of units and any unit of measurement. The end result should be a bar graph that you can discuss as a group.

How Far Did It Roll? Measured with _____					
10					
9					
8					
7					
6					
5					
4					
3					
2					
1					
Object					

Try It!

Does a heavier car go farther than a lighter car? Get two cars that are the same size, shape, and weight. (They don't have to be the same color.) Tape weights to one of the cars. See if making the car heavier makes it go farther.

I am measuring my car's path in _____.

	Car with 0 weights	Car with 1 weight	Car with 2 weights	Car with 3 weights	Car with 4 weights
Distance in _____					

Dear Families:

This week we are studying things that **roll**. We are testing all sorts of things, from balls and blocks to toy cars. It's easy to extend these activities at home.

Set up anything for a ramp. It could be a piece of wood, a cookie sheet, or an ironing board. And then encourage your child to try testing things at home. (Of course, think about safety and breakage. Something that would break at the end of the roll, such as an egg, wouldn't be a good choice—unless you'd like to try a new way of scrambling eggs.)

Classification is a key skill for early childhood. This activity is ideal for practicing sorting. Ask your child to make two piles of things: those that roll and those that don't.

Another way we ask children to think like scientists is asking them to **predict** and then test a prediction. Making piles of things that roll is a step in modeling. It's like building a theory of how things work in the world. Models help us predict.

Find a new object that your child hasn't tested yet. Ask, "What do you think? Will it roll?" And then ask, "Why do you think that?" (Patience! It may take time for those modeling thoughts to come out as words.)

Then, of course, do the test. Remember, experimenting isn't really about being right or wrong. It's about persistence. So always remind your child to try again.

We'll also read about the man who invented the safety helmet. He called it a "Hard Boiled Hat." Remind your young bikers to always wear their helmets!

Thanks for being great STEM partners. And have fun.

E. W. Bullard: STEM Star

E. W. Bullard was a soldier. He wore a metal hat to protect his head when he was at war.

His father had a factory. The factory made soft helmets for workers.

When E. W. came home from the war, he told his father how to make a better helmet.

He called the new hat a "Hard Boiled Hat." It was stronger. It protected heads better.

Race car drivers wear helmets. Bicycle riders wear helmets. Baseball players wear helmets.

Who else wears a helmet? _____

_____

_____

_____

When should you wear a helmet? _____

_____

_____

_____

Slipping, Sliding

The Big Question: What Force Makes Things Slow Down When They Are Moving?

Creating Context

While young children may not use the term "**friction**," the idea of it is probably well within their experience. They slip on ice, on sand, or into puddles because friction is low. Gooey objects fall from their hands. In colder climates, sleds and skates provide winter fun on surfaces with less friction. In this lesson, children explore the force of friction by observing the time it takes to go down a standard **slide**. The resistance of the slide to the movement of the slider is something children can both feel and measure. They also begin to think quantitatively about forces by using a simple counting device to measure the time of a slide. This activity continues the beginning experiences with friction in unit 4.

TEACHER TIP

Almost all mobile phones have stopwatch features these days, and, of course, that method of timing is more accurate. But we've recommended an instrument with an audible click here for two reasons: the counts are more recognizable, and the learner, rather than the device, is responsible for the counting.

Engage

Prepare for the following exploration by telling children they are going to become clocks! Using a metronome with a distinct click, have children practice counting aloud together. Use this method to time some familiar things for practice. For example, how long does it take to walk down the hall, to empty a bottle of water, or to pick up toys? Use the metronome for cars on a ramp. In the following exploration, you will use this same counting method to measure the time it takes for a child to go down a slide. (Very few slides will require counting past ten.)

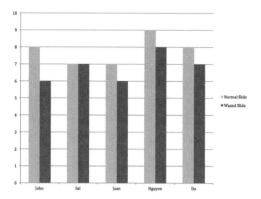

Explore

Take a field trip to the playground. Ask volunteers to go down the slide. Using the children as counters, measure the time of the slide. Older children can learn to do an average by doing the same observation twice, adding the two, and dividing the sum in half. Older children might also help younger peers create bar graphs of the averages to show how long different students took to go down the slide.

Can you reduce the **friction**? Make the slide smoother by rubbing it with waxed paper. Have the children try **sliding** again.

Explain

When you go down a **slide**, there are forces speeding you up and slowing you down. Gravity makes you go down. The slide pushes up on you. Air and the rough surface create **friction**,which slows you down. When you come to the bottom of the slide, you hit the landing surface, which pushes you to a stop. Wax can make the surface smoother. It changes one of the forces: friction. It reduces friction from the slide's surface.

Elaborate

If there is very little friction between things, they slip. We have to walk carefully on snow, ice, or wet ground. Batters and archers wrap the handles of their bats and bows with rough tape to increase the friction under their grips. Athletes can run faster or jump higher if their shoes have good friction.

Invite children to observe the different sorts of soles that shoes can have. Ask children to sit along a wall with their feet out and compare the soles of the shoes they wear to school. Then recruit any adults you can find. Are their shoes different? Ask families to help as well, comparing types of shoes. This can happen at home (comparing dress shoes, track shoes, golf shoes, and others) or on a trip to a shoe store.

Using a collection of photos of shoes, ask children to choose a good kind of shoe for different environments:

- snow and ice

- a running track

- a dance floor

- a soccer field

Shoes in different places on the earth are very different! Children might have special examples of shoes from their ancestors—Native American moccasins, dancing clogs, or ornamental shoes from Thailand. And here's a fun fact: the word "sabotage" comes from a time when people stuck their wooden shoes—sabots—into machines to break them!

Evaluate

Using a picture of a slide, help children think about the forces acting on a sliding child. Emphasize the senses; children shouldn't be expected to know anything theoretically. Put arrows on the picture—down for gravity, up for the force of the slide pushing on the slider. (These are not formal vectors that a physics student might use to show force and direction, but simply representations of the forces the students can sense.)

Integrate

This activity uses a musical metronome as a timing device. Note that CCSS and NGSS ask that children learn that natural movements like sliding can be measured. At this level, it is not necessary to achieve a high level of accuracy. While there are many devices with more sophisticated technology than a metronome (including most mobile phones), a metronome that can be observed with the senses is more developmentally appropriate.

That same metronome can, of course, be used for music. Use it to time the singing of a familiar song—slower, then faster. Use the terms "slower" and "faster" to prepare children for the use of the same terms in subsequent physical science activities.

👀 EARLY EXPLORERS

Find a sidewalk with grass alongside it. Have a contest to see on which surface a ball will roll farther. Allow children to suggest other places in their learning space that would be good to roll balls (tile, gym flooring, carpet, running track), and then allow them to try rolling them there.

If your program has a custodian who uses a sign to indicate a wet floor, ask the custodian to explain it. Ask children to physically model what might happen if they slipped on that wet floor and how to walk safely.

Safety Note

The base of any piece of playground equipment should have a safety surface. Some playgrounds use synthetic wood chips or rubberized surfaces made from recycled tires. If you have doubts about the proper installation of playground equipment, ask the insurance specialist at your school, program, or city parks department.

Ask children to feel the safety surface under the swings and slides. The children might notice its elasticity. Some safety surfaces are made of tiny cubes of rubber from old tires or shreds of recycled rubber.

Then ask children to write a story about a sliding experience that has a beginning, middle, and end.

In *Thud! Wile E. Coyote Experiments with Forces and Motion*, author Mark Weakland takes a whimsical look at forces and motion. But the science is correct, and the way in which the dialogue encourages prediction and analysis is great. Wile E. Coyote's "desert surfer" slows down because of friction. Ask a child to safely demonstrate that a skateboard doesn't go on forever with one kick. Then ask children to feel the wheels. (They may be slightly warm.)

More Literature to Integrate

In *Motion: Push and Pull, Fast and Slow*, Darlene Stille asks children to explore the surfaces in their school or home and predict what will slow down motion (which have more friction), such as running shoes, sleds, bicycle tires, and baking sheets. In this book, children find an experiment comparing the force needed to drag an object over different surfaces using an elastic band to measure force.

Content Background

Friction is a force that usually acts in the opposite direction of an object's movement. It is most easily understood as the resistance of one surface with respect to another. A scientist might go deeper, describing the electrostatic forces between particles in two objects. In the content background for unit 4, we described four kinds of friction:

- static friction, which would keep your shoes on the sidewalk or help you climb a rock wall

- sliding friction, in which one surface passes over another, like moving a box across a floor

- rolling friction, which affects a ball on a surface

- fluid friction, which slows the movement of a solid through a liquid

In the world of young children, rolling and **sliding** friction will be the easiest to observe with their senses. Athletes want very high static friction on their shoes most of the time (as in the engineering challenge). But dancers want to slide across the floor, so dance shoes may be very smooth, and some dance studios even put slippery powders on the dance floor to reduce sliding friction. Skates slide because the pressure of the blade melts the water a little bit underneath it.

Young children can easily compare surfaces to decide which are smoother and classify them as to whether they will have more or less friction. Some surfaces, like tracks, may have tiny bits of rubber or rough asphalt that children can actually see with simple hand lenses. Combined with the "bumps" (cleats) on track shoes, they help a runner's legs create strong pushes as the athlete moves along.

Sample Common Core Standards

Write narratives in which they recount two or more appropriately sequenced events, include some details regarding what happened, use temporal words to signal event order, and provide some sense of closure. (CCSS. ELA-Literacy.W.1.3) (CCSS Initiative 2016a, 19)

Tell and write time from analog and digital clocks to the nearest five minutes, using a.m. and p.m. (CCSS.Math.Content.2.MD.C.7) (CCSS Initiative 2016b, 20)

Engineering Challenge

Using the following activity, encourage children to explore the friction created by different kinds of shoes on different surfaces. Children can think of ways to make shoes slip less, then explain why their ideas make shoes safer.

Dear Families:

More pushes and pulls this week! We are studying how **friction** can slow down something that is **sliding**. While children may not know the word "friction," they can feel the effects of friction. And when friction is very low, children know that slipping and sliding can happen.

One way we are exploring friction is to compare the soles of people's shoes. Most children wear athletic shoes with rubber soles. The friction between the shoe and the floor is pretty high.

When golfers or baseball players want good shoes, they look for very rough soles! They may buy shoes with cleats to dig into the soil so that the shoes don't slip at all.

But when we go dancing, we want our feet to slide. And at a party, we might wear a shoe with a metal heel.

Can you help our study of friction by helping your child observe shoes and their soles? You might do it at home or take a walk through the shoe department of a store. Ask, "Which shoes are slippery? Which shoes will help you keep from slipping?" Just as we did last week, classifying items such as shoes into groups is a great skill to practice.

Thanks for being great STEM partners. And have fun!

Try It!

First, measure the time it takes to go down a slide.

We can count together using a tool that makes a loud click. The tool is called a metronome. Musicians use it to help keep the beat in a song. We need to practice because it is difficult to measure something quick like a slider.

Then we'll try to make the slide slippery. We can use a special paper with wax on it or spray wax on the slide.

Can wax make the push of friction less? Try it.

 TEACHER TIP

We've included several ways to maintain data here. Counting, averaging, and making histograms are appropriate for different ages. Remember that the object is to learn to collect data to make an argument, so high accuracy is less important than the concept that pushes and pulls can be measured.

Student	Counts on Slide	Counts on Slippery Slide

Student	Slide 1—No Wax	Slide 2—No Wax	Slide 3—Waxed	Slide 4—Waxed
	Add the two counts and divide in half.		Add the two counts and divide in half.	
	Add the two counts and divide in half.		Add the two counts and divide in half.	

(continued on next page)

(continued from previous page)

Student	Slide 1—No Wax	Slide 2—No Wax	Slide 3—Waxed	Slide 4—Waxed
	Add the two counts and divide in half. _____		Add the two counts and divide in half. _____	
	Add the two counts and divide in half. _____		Add the two counts and divide in half. _____	

Counts					
10					
9					
8					
7					
6					
5					
4					
3					
2					
1					
Student					

Be an Engineer!

Sometimes we want to make sure things do not slip.

Special shoes might be good for an icy hill.

Track shoes help a runner push to start fast.

Think of a way to make a shoe slip less.

Draw the new shoe!

Pretend you are selling your shoe to a friend. Why should they buy your safer shoe?

_____

_____

_____

_____

_____

Help Lauren Explain Her Slide

Gravity pulls me _____.

I feel _____ when I slide down.

Friction makes me go _____.

At the bottom of the slide, I stop because _____

_____

_____

_____.

Adi and Rudi Dassler: STEM Stars

Once shoes were made of cloth, leather, or wood. But Adolf and Rudolf had a better idea.

They made shoes of rubber with cleats. They were for sports.

They started making shoes in their mother's basement. People loved the shoes.

Why would a shoe with bumps on the bottom be better?

Adi and Rudi made thousands of rubber shoes together. But then they had a fight!

Adi started a new company called Adidas.

Rudi called his new company Puma.

David Beckham wears Adidas when he plays soccer.

Usain Bolt wears Pumas when he runs.

What kind of shoes do you like best? _____

_____

Why? _____

_____

How could you test them? _____

_____

What's the Matter?

The Big Question: How Can We Compare the Properties of Solids and Liquids?

Creating Context

Matter is all around us. We can touch, feel, and taste it. The properties of matter help us identify what kind of matter it is. Words like "heavy," "light," "hard," and "soft" are important ways to identify types of matter.

Matter can be a **solid**, **liquid**, or gas. It is easiest for young children to use their senses to identify the properties of solids and liquids and classify these types of matter. But gases have identifiable properties as well. In this unit, children begin with solids and liquids, building observational skills for their observation of gases later.

 TEACHER TIP

Students begin to compare **solid** and **liquid** forms of matter in this unit. A limited discussion of air—a gas—will occur later. The emphasis should be on properties that children can check out with their own senses. Review senses in this unit and emphasize arguing through evidence. Use claim, evidence, and reasoning even if you don't use those specific terms: "What do you think? What's your evidence? What makes you think that?"

Sample Next Generation Science Standards

Disciplinary Core Ideas

PS1.A: Structure and Properties of Matter

- Different kinds of matter exist and many of them can be either solid or liquid, depending on temperature. Matter can be described and classified by its observable properties. (2-PS1-1)
- Different properties are suited to different purposes. (2-PS1-2, 2-PS1-3)

Performance Expectation

Students who demonstrate understanding can:

Plan and conduct an investigation to describe and classify different kinds of materials by their observable properties. (2-PS1-1)

(NGSS Lead States 2013)

Engage

In *What Is the World Made Of?* Kathleen Weidner Zoehfeld discusses the three states of matter. Comparing **solids** and **liquids**, the author asks, "Have you ever seen anyone walk through a wall? Did you ever drink a glass of blocks? Have you ever played with a lemonade doll, or put on milk for socks?" (2013, 4–5). Read the book to page 18, or go to the book's website to hear a sample. Then ask children to invent their own silly questions, which use solids for liquids and liquids for solids. (You can use the remainder of the book in the next unit.)

Explore

Begin by exploring the properties of solids. Ask children to find out how many small ice cubes can be added to a cylindrical glass. Mark how high the ice is with a wax pencil or tape. Then let the ice melt and ask the children how much more space there is, or how much more water can fit in the glass. Make another mark. Ask children to explain what they see. Some children may be able to observe that the ice cubes are stiff or solid and have empty spaces between them. Some children may describe how the water fills up the empty spaces between the cubes.

Explain

Liquids can change shape, but **solids** normally do not. Put ice cubes in a glass. Look at how much space they take up. Mark the side of the glass. Then let them melt. How much space does the liquid take up? Ask children to explain to a friend why they think the amount of space changed. (There is extra space between the cubes that children can see, because cubes have a specific shape.)

Introduce the terms "solid," "liquid," "melting," and "freezing." Water can be solid or liquid. Heat makes ice melt. Some foods, like breakfast cereal, contain both solids and liquid.

Elaborate

Freeze equal amounts of water in two nonlatex gloves. Put one nonlatex glove inside a fabric glove or mitten. Let the two ice-filled gloves sit in a warm place for an hour or more. After an hour, which has melted more? Depending on the

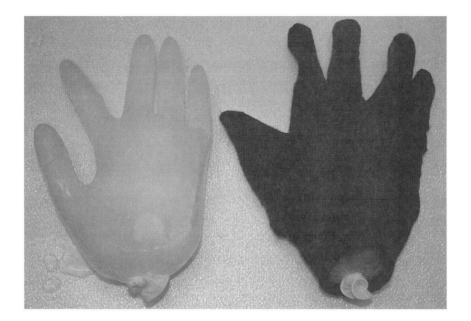

developmental age of the children, there are lots of ways to measure melting. Students can simply draw around the remaining icy fingers, measure the water in the glove, or weigh the remaining ice. Ask children to decide how they will measure. Then discuss why it is important to wear the right clothing in cold weather.

Content Background

A **solid** is a form of matter that takes up space and has a definite shape and volume. A **liquid** takes up space but takes the shape of the container it is in. A gas is a form of matter that takes up space. A gas has no shape and no constant volume. While a gas is often invisible, it also has properties that children can sense. All forms of matter have mass; they are attracted by Earth's gravity and so have weight.

Melting and freezing are changes of state that occur in all matter. They are related to the energy between particles. The particles in solids maintain a relatively constant distance from one another, while those of liquids can move more freely relative to one another. The particles in gases have the most energy and therefore have the most freedom to move relative to one another.

Heat is a form of energy. Changes in temperature are the result of changes in energy, but another result of a change in energy can be change of state—such as from solid to liquid or liquid to gas.

Water is a unique substance with very high levels of electrostatic force between its particles. Positive and negative charges cause some particles to

 **EARLY EXPLORERS**

Make an ice person out of ice cream, ice cubes, or a Popsicle and let it melt. Ask children to act out what the ice person might say as it melts. Photograph the object periodically and post where the children can see, so that children can tell the story of the changes that occur. Ask, "Could we find a safe spot for our ice person?" If children suggest a refrigerator or outside on a cold day, let them try.

attract and others to repel. In water, the slightly negative oxygen atom is attracted to the slightly positive hydrogen atoms of other molecules. These forces are greater as water cools; the molecules are in very specific positions in ice-forming crystals.

Also, water expands when it freezes, unlike most substances, which simply get denser as they get colder. That's also a result of the charges between the particles. It takes a lot more energy to change water from solid to liquid to gas than it takes for other liquids. Many of these ideas will be introduced later. In the sense of NGSS, they are beyond the assessment limits of this unit. But building a foundation of good sensory experiences that children discuss with one another is important. The idea that water can be a solid, a liquid, or a gas can be explored at the early childhood level.

A common misconception among children is that a glove warms a hand or melts ice. The glove is an insulator, made of a material that is a bit more resistant to heat passing through it. If children suggest that a glove is warm, let them put a thermometer into a dry glove at room temperature. This is another sort of side trip that pays off in later understanding.

Evaluate

Create a place where children can classify the properties and examples of common materials as solids or liquids. This can be done with actual materials for younger children, using tables with labels or pictures, using a whiteboard or a Venn diagram drawn on a floor or playground area. Older children can begin with the examples in the Try It! activity (page 92) and then expand by using old magazines, the Internet, or cameras. If you set up a display of solids and liquids, make sure to save room to add gases (like a balloon) later.

Sample Common Core Standards

Use words and phrases acquired through conversations, reading and being read to, and responding to texts, including using adjectives and adverbs to describe. (CCSS. ELA-Literacy.L.2.6) (CCSS Initiative 2016a, 27)

Directly compare two objects with a measurable attribute in common, to see which object has "more of"/"less of" the attribute, and describe the difference. (CCSS.Math.Content.K.MD.A.2) (CCSS Initiative 2016b, 12)

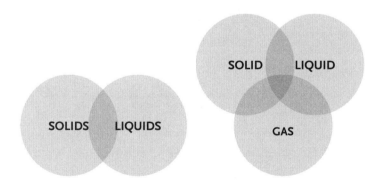

Integrate

The Poetry of Science, an anthology edited by Sylvia Vardell and Janet Wong (2015), contains many poems you can use to enhance both language arts and science. Read the poem "Antarctica, Antarctic O!" by Heidi Bee Roemer aloud. Every time children hear an "O," have them give a signal (hands raised or mouths forming "O").

Antarctica!

by Heidi Bee Roemer

I'm cOld as a SnOw KOne,
My tOes are like lead.
My ears? They're both frOzen.
My nOse? ROsy red.
As pOlar winds blOw,

I'm chilled to the bOne,
The thermometer tells me
What I should have knOwn—
It's zerO degrees
…I wish I'd stayed hOme.

"Antarctica!" by Heidi Bee Roemer; copyright © 2012 by Heidi Bee Roemer. Used by permission of the author, who controls all rights. First appeared in *The Poetry Friday Anthology*® by Sylvia Vardell and Janet Wong (Pomelo Books).

More Literature to Integrate

- Vicki Cobb's *I Get Wet* includes Cobb's characteristic open-ended activities and dialogue all about water.

- Paul A. Reynolds's *Sidney and Simon: Full Steam Ahead!* offers many authentic examples of liquids and their properties.

Engineering Challenge

Engineers often do product testing to compare quality and economy. Using the following activity, allow children to compare the insulating value of gloves in a product test and then develop their own oral commercial for the gloves they find are best.

Safety Note

Young children should never use unshielded glass thermometers. You can purchase special school thermometers with plastic backing at low cost.

Some schools, early childhood programs, or homes may still have old mercury thermometers stored somewhere. These should be sent to a regulated disposal center and never used.

Be an Engineer!

Gloves are a very important part of winter wear.

They keep our hands warm. They keep us healthy.

Can you compare gloves?

Which gloves can keep your hands warmer?

A thermometer can measure temperature.

Put thermometers inside different gloves. Put the gloves in a refrigerator or put ice on top of them. (Be fair! Use the same number of cubes for each glove.)

How long should you wait? _____

_____

When you are done, which glove is warmer inside? _____

_____

Dear Families:

The matter around us can be **solid**, **liquid**, or **gas**. This week we are comparing the properties of solids and liquids. Your children can learn a lot about matter with their senses.

Many foods and cooking experiences can help children understand solids and liquids. Cook with your children. As you do, you can discuss the following concepts:

- Water goes from liquid to solid when it freezes.
- Popsicles melt from solid to liquid in your mouth.
- Liquid cake or pancake batter and eggs become solid when they are cooked.
- Gelatin can go from liquid to solid and then to liquid again.

We are also looking at how liquids can take on the shape of their container. Pouring an interesting liquid from a glass to a cup to another glass can be the start of a great conversation. When young children see a liquid poured from a small glass to a larger one (where the level will be lower), they often believe that there is less of the liquid in the larger glass. Pouring the liquid back and forth can spark some great conversations.

Using the methods of engineers, we are comparing gloves to see which work best to keep hands warm. If you have any odd gloves you can lend for our tests, we'd appreciate them! We will also be reminding your scientists that it's important to wear the right clothing in cold weather to stay healthy and safe.

We will read about the invention of the ice cream maker. Ice cream goes from liquid to solid, and if you wait long enough, it goes from solid back to liquid again. Have a cone for the sake of STEM.

Thanks for being great STEM partners. And have fun.

Try It!

Properties of Solids	Properties of Liquids

Examples of Solids	Examples of Liquids

Discuss the following words with children. Challenge the children to put each word in the appropriate space(s) in the chart or in a Venn diagram chalked onto the floor or pavement.

hard	visible	sugar cube	gelatin
soft	invisible	syrup	egg white
shaped	cool	ice	cooked egg
no shape	heavy	water	
warm	light	gelatin solution	

Nancy Johnson: STEM Star

Do you like ice cream? Once, only very rich people could have it.

Many years ago, before your great-great-great-grandparents were born, Nancy Johnson invented a machine. After that, with cream, some salt, and a little ice, anyone could make ice cream.

An ice cream machine has an outer bucket and a smaller bowl inside. Ice and salt go on the outside of the smaller bowl. The cream goes on the inside. Then you crank and crank. The cream becomes a solid. Cream is a liquid. But ice cream is a solid. People loved ice cream, so they didn't mind the work!

Ice cream needs flavors. Name as many flavors of ice cream as you can. Then find out where these flavors come from. Here's a hint for one: chocolate comes from a plant that grows in rain forests.

_____

_____

_____

_____

_____

_____

Drop by Drop

The Big Question: What Are the Properties of Water?

Creating Context

Water is all around. It is the essence of life and a source of endless play. But it is also great science, since it exists as **solid**, **liquid**, and **gas** in environments within the sensory reach of young children. In unit 6, children compared solids and liquids. They used consistent terms such as "heavy," "light," "hard," and "soft" to describe the properties of solids and liquids. Young children can use the same sort of consistent vocabulary as they continue to explore the properties of water. This unit will include new ideas about how water behaves when it is a solid, a liquid, and even a gas.

Engage

Prepare a variety of containers and ask children to predict which will hold water. (Include some paper containers; some plastic, cloth, or metal; and some with small or large pores such as sieves, colanders, and strainers.) Once children have sorted the containers they think will hold water from those they think will not, ask them to test their predictions. Make sure it is a fair test. Put the same amount of water in each container—ideally, a small ketchup cup full. Then classify.

Explore

In unit 6, children learned that water is a liquid. Liquids can take the shape of any container. They have a specific volume but no specific shape. But water is also a special sort of

TEACHER TIP

The ability to understand conservation of volume was one of the key ideas that Jean Piaget used to describe the cognitive development of young children. Unit 6 introduced the idea of conservation as children observed melting ice in the last unit. Children also poured liquids from one type of container to another and discussed how much could fit.

In appendix D, a video on the Piagetian interviews about conservation shows how children of different ages might understand conservation. As you watch the video and your own group of children, pay special attention to dialogue that helps children think about their own thinking.

Take a walk around your learning area and look for signs of water—puddles, dew or condensation, taps and toilets, buckets and bottles. Some children may not recognize at first that each different example is actually water. Ask, "How do you know it's water?" They might suggest that it flows, that it is clear, or that it forms drops. Be sure to caution children not to taste the water they find. You can post photos of water in various forms as children become more observant.

substance that sticks to itself. The forces in water can make it form drops.

Give children plastic eyedroppers. Begin by asking them to put drops on waxed paper. Discuss how they must not squirt the water but let it drop. This will take practice and patience—plan for the time. Challenge the children to make a line of drops or a circle of drops. They can also make a pattern by placing a line drawing under the waxed paper.

Next, ask children to describe the shape of a drop as it falls from the eyedropper. When children are able to let the water drop because of its own weight, ask them to count how many drops fill a tiny container such as a ketchup cup. (This activity works best in pairs, with one child counting and another using the dropper.) Make sure the children respond to your "no squirting" direction before they begin.

Add a tiny bit of dish soap to the water and try again. Are the soapy drops different as they fall from the eyedropper? Are they different on the waxed paper?

Explain

Water can be a **solid**, **liquid**, or **gas**. It can be in the air or in tiny drops on the surface of a glass or window. It can even come from our breath. Show children ice, which has a shape and a size, and liquid water, which has a size but no shape. (You might repeat the ice-melting experience from unit 6 in a different container.)

Then ask children if there could be water in the air. Ask them to blow on a cool mirror or window. If you live in a northern climate, children may recall when the water in their breath became visible on a very cold day. Ask, "How did the water get there?"

Elaborate

Give children metal soup cans (from which sharp edges and labels have been removed). Put very cold water or a mixture of water and ice in the cans, and then ask children to observe the moisture that condenses on the outside of the cans. (Ice in the water can make this happen faster.) Children may want to write their initials in the condensation.

Ask students where the water drops on the outside of the cans came from. Many children will believe that the drops come from inside the can rather than from the air. Next, ask the children how they can test their ideas. One way is to repeat the activity above, using colored water inside the can. The drops outside the can won't be colored.

Evaluate

Provide the children a new set of containers like those they tested in the first engagement exercise—sieves, sand sifters, colanders, paper and plastic cups (some with holes punched in the bottom), eyedroppers, hollow coffee stirrers, and straws. Ask the children to predict those that will hold water and those that won't.

Integrate

Chris Barton's book *Whoosh! Lonnie Johnson's Super-Soaking Stream of Inventions* is the story of an unemployed engineer who makes his fortune by inventing the Super Soaker. Read the book to the class, emphasizing the frustrations, failures, and perseverance of Lonnie Johnson. When you get to the foldout of the squirt gun, take out a squirt gun. Then review vocabulary from previous units: What pushes the water? What forces are involved? Why does the water eventually fall?

by Vicki Cobb illustrated by Julia Gorton

More Literature to Integrate

- Vicki Cobb's classic book *I Get Wet!* is an interactive book you can read aloud and alternate with physical experiences. Like her other books for this level, the dialogue is great to emulate.

- Paul A. Reynolds's book *Sydney and Simon: Full Steam Ahead!* includes fun text, experiments with condensation like the one mentioned in this unit, and age-appropriate mathematics integration.

- April Pulley Sayre's *Raindrops Roll* has outstanding photographs of water droplets in diverse places and contexts. It can provide a great observational opportunity to help children recognize water all over.

- Ashley Spires's *The Most Magnificent Thing* describes the invention of a new toy. So does Gilbert Ford's *The Marvelous Thing That Came from a Spring*. These books can be good accompaniments to any activity in which you ask children to invent better toys.

Content Background

Water is a unique material, with properties that are directly related to its molecular structure. None of this chemistry is appropriate at the early childhood level—and yet the interesting properties that result from water's structure can be observed, measured, and used to create arguments from evidence at this level. To generate even more good questions, they can also be connected to things children see every day.

Water adheres to itself because it's polar. That means the electrical charges in a water molecule are unbalanced; positive ends of one molecule are attracted to negative ends of another. This attraction is greater at lower temperatures. That chemistry isn't relevant to young learners, but their observations may lead them to the (almost true) observation that water is "sticky." It forms drops and beads, extends across small spaces such as fine sieves, and climbs inside of tiny straws or stir sticks. That's why a small sieve can sometimes hold a little water even though it has holes in it. That's also what happens when drops form at the end of a water dropper.

If water is allowed to fall slowly from a small tube, each drop will be about the same size. From a chemical perspective, that's because there is a specific point (mass) at which the forces holding the water molecules together are less than the pull of gravity. Again, that chemistry idea isn't important to the explorations. To the young chemist, the observable property is that similar-size drops form. Because water may adhere to a surface, it might go up a tiny straw or coffee stirrer and not fall out.

Detergent (soap) is a molecule that has two different ends: One is hydrophilic. That means it is attracted to the water. But the other end is attracted to fats. In a dishpan, soap separates water from grease. In a dropper, it makes water a little less able to bead up.

In the next unit, children will discover that water heats and cools much more slowly than most other materials. Chemists say water has a high "specific heat." The observable property for young children is that water can cool an object or a living thing.

Engineering Challenge

In the previous unit, children explored the value of gloves to insulate (prevent energy from passing from a warm space to a cold space). In this challenge, children must invent a wrapping to keep a cold drink cold. They might use some of the same materials they used for the egg drop activity in unit 2 (such as bubble wrap, paper, cloth, leather, or any other wrapper that is handy).

If you have safe thermometers that fit in the openings of soda cans, you can use them. (Fill with water and refrigerate to start.) If you need larger openings, safely remove the top of a soup can. Use larger cans like those from crushed tomatoes as the outer limit of the package. By using two cans, one large and one small, you can modify the activity so that children can put sand, packing peanuts, or small manipulatives in the space to create insulation. (Remember to use safe thermometers.)

Try It!

Put some water in your dropper.

Hold the dropper up. Let the water fall. Look carefully!

What does a drop look like?

Draw your drop:

Put your drops on waxed paper. Do they look the same? _____

Make a path of drops.

Get a little cup.

How many drops fit in the cup? _____

Let a friend count them for you.

Try some soapy water.

How many drops fit in the cup? _____

Last, put some water in a can.

Put some ice in it. Stir. Watch for drops of water on the outside of the can. Where did the water come from?

_____

How could you see if you were right?_____

_____

_____

Be an Engineer!

Some materials can act like gloves. They can keep warm things warm and cold things cold.

Some people stay at the beach all day. They want to keep their soda cool. Can you invent a good package to keep the soda cool?

_____

_____

What did you put around the can? _____

Could it be like a glove? _____

Could it be like an egg package? _____

Take the temperature of your drink after one hour. What is the temperature? _____

Whose can stayed coolest? _____

Engineers try again and again. How could you improve your package?_____

_____

_____

_____

Dear Families:

This week we are studying water. It's all around us—a special substance that can be **solid**, **liquid**, or **gas**. Most of our body is made of water. Without water, nothing on Earth could live.

Water is also the easiest material to study. We will begin by seeing what can hold water. You can do this at home. Group things that can hold water (such as cups, pans, and bottles) and things that cannot hold water (such as colanders and coffee filters). Have a big towel ready when your scientists begin to test. Take a plastic cup, poke some holes in the bottom, and test it again. Most children will be able to sort the things that clearly can hold water from those that cannot. But there are some things in between. A fine-mesh kitchen strainer might hold a little water for a little time. You can pick up a little water in a thin straw, and it will stay there for a while, too. (Secret: That's because water is "cohesive" and has a tendency to stick to itself in drops.)

We are also looking at the shape of water drops and the places that water condenses around our daily environment. Take a walk with your child inside or outside your home to find water drops and condensation. You might have water condense on the windshield of your car if the air outside is warm and your car is blowing cooler air inside.

Finally, look for the water inside us. Breathe on a mirror or a cool window. Remember our patter: "What do you see or feel? Why do you think this is there?" Every answer is a good one.

Our engineering challenge is to design a package to keep a can of soda cold. If you use a thermos or a cooler, show it to your child.

Thanks for being great STEM partners. And have fun!

From *Teaching STEM Literacy: A Constructivist Approach* by Juliana Texley and Ruth M. Ruud © 2018. Published by Redleaf Press, www.redleafpress.org. This page may be reproduced for classroom use only.

Lonnie Johnson: STEM Star

Lonnie Johnson loved to build things.

He built a robot for a science fair.

He powered a NASA probe.

But his favorite invention was a toy—he made the Super Soaker!

It wasn't easy. First Lonnie had to make the toy. It wasn't perfect. So he made it better. He had to get people to buy it. He knew people could have fun with it.

What is your favorite toy?

Draw it here:

How could you make it better? _____

_____

_____

Why will your new toy be more fun? _____

_____

It's in the Air

The Big Question: How Can We Use Our Senses to Find Out about Air?

Creating Context

Air is matter, just like the solids and liquids around us that are easier to see. Air is a mixture of different kinds of gas. It can be any **shape** and can fill any space. Air is almost always invisible. But we can sense it. Air has properties, including **weight**, just like the solids and liquids that are all around us. It's easier for young children to describe the properties of solids and liquids than to describe the properties of gases, but the ideas and practices that learners use to describe solids and liquids can be extended to describing air.

Engage

Begin by blowing bubbles. Ask, "What's inside the bubble?" Allow children to speculate. This is actually a difficult question for children. Any answer is appropriate. Record some of the children's ideas on the board or in a voice recorder.

Blow up some balloons. Bounce them around. Then ask again, "What's inside?" You can repeat this process with a beach ball, a soccer ball, or even a blown-up nonlatex glove.

Explore

Review solids, liquids, and gases with a classic experiment. Fill a clear eight-ounce plastic cup with clear, sparkling, freshly opened soda. Reviewing terms from unit 6, ask if the soda is a solid or liquid.

 TEACHER TIP

Some early childhood researchers believe that children should look only at the properties of solid and liquid matter in their STEM investigations. We've taken a different approach. Since the effects of **air** are all around, we believe that children can use their senses to make the same sorts of conclusions about air as they do with solids and liquids. The key is to use similar terms for similar ideas, such as "heavy" and "light." But remember, this will be only the beginning of children's understanding. The purpose of these explorations is to look at cross-cutting concepts that allow us to identify materials by properties like **size**, **shape**, and **weight**, not to become air experts.

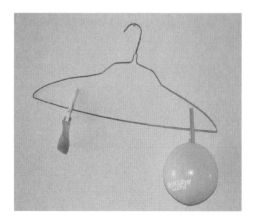

Then take out one or two fresh raisins. Ask again, "What type of matter is a raisin? How do you know a raisin is solid and the soda is liquid?" (Answer: raisins have **shape**.) Then ask, "What are the bubbles?"

Drop the raisins in the soda. Ask children to observe carefully and then explain what they see to a friend.

Compare the bubbles in the soda to the bubbles children saw in the "Engage" phase of the unit. Could the same thing be in both kinds of bubbles? Do the bubbles go up or down? Are they heavy or light? Do they stick to the raisins or bounce off them? Do they all have the same shape?

Explain

After children have developed their own ideas and explained them to a friend, summarize their arguments and emphasize common terms to describe this new form of matter: a gas.

- Can air take up space? (It is in the bubbles, balls, and balloons.)

- Can air be light? (Soda bubbles go up.)

- Can air push or pull? (Try making a fan with paper.)

Elaborate

Can air be heavy? We can demonstrate that **air** can be heavy by using a simple demonstration from Vicki Cobb's classic book *I Face the Wind*. Give each group of children two small balloons. Ask them to put air into one but not the other. Then ask them to see which balloon is heavier by clipping each to one end of a simple clothes hanger. Hang the hanger from a hook, string, or anywhere it can hang freely. Which balloon is heavier?

Evaluate

Modify the Venn diagram used in unit 6 or use a concept map. Ask children to compare the properties of solids, liquids, and gases. For the youngest scientists, Venn diagrams are an ideal way to draw big and respond in a kinesthetic way. Use sidewalk chalk to create large spaces for each category. Use cards for key words like "**weight**," "**size**," and "**shape**."

Put some solids in one space, put some liquids in another, and in the third put balloons full of **air**—a gas. Then ask volunteers to identify things that have a definite shape (solids) or things that have size but no special shape (liquids), either by pointing or moving to that space. You might ask, "Which space has things that can change shape but have a size?"

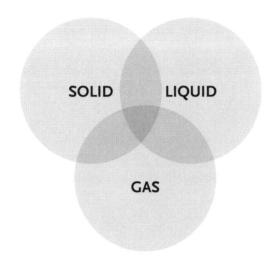

 **EARLY EXPLORERS**

Look for air currents or wind around your learning environment. In a walk around the area, children can carry feathers on strings. Blowing bubbles also reveals breeze and wind. Do the bubbles fall down or float away?

Children can make their own wind through straws to move another child's feather or a Ping-Pong ball across a table. Emphasize that wind can push. Can it pull? Open a door quickly and watch what happens to the feather or bubbles.

Integrate

Emily Morgan's *Next Time You See a Maple Seed* is a guide to observation with many facts about the movement of these objects in the air. From observing the samaras, children can infer facts about air. This book is ideal to use at a station where children can continue to play with the samaras. (Waxing or pressing them in a book can preserve them.) Compare the movement of the samara to that of a paper helicopter. Then ask children to imagine the helicopter that Leonardo da Vinci imagined.

Michelle Worthington's *Noah Chases the Wind* is a story about a child's use of his senses to identify the wind he cannot see. It is a great way to review how our senses can help us identify the properties of matter.

More Literature to Integrate

- In *Every Breath We Take: A Book about Air*, Maya Ajmera and Dominique Browning ask beginning scientists to think about the invisible air all around them. In the middle of the book, the authors write, "Clean air is invisible. But you know it is there" (2016, 14). That's a great invitation to asking students, "How do you know?" before experimenting.

- Laurence Anholt's *Leonardo and the Flying Boy* is a story for children ages four to eight about the artist Leonardo da Vinci and his imaginary apprentice. Biographies like this can help children see themselves as STEM Stars.

- *I Face the Wind* by Vicki Cobb is full of open dialogue and simple activities to allow young children to explore the properties of air in an interactive way. The dialogue in the book, like others from Cobb, invites modeling. The balloon demonstration in this unit is adapted from this book.

- Melissa Stewart's *Feathers: Not Just for Flying* is a book about both nature and engineering. As a read-aloud, it offers special opportunities for dialogue. The last four pages emphasize feathers' ability to reduce friction and to lift using the force of air, allowing you to emphasize crosscutting concepts and extend the vocabulary of previous lessons, such as "push" and "friction."

- A great physical science poem by Janet Wong appears on page 110. Her book with Sylvia Vardell, *The Poetry of Science*, is listed in appendix A and appendix D.

Content Background

The basic properties of solids, liquids, and gases are important core ideas in early childhood science. While NGSS recommends emphasizing solids and liquids, the **air** all around children is impossible for them to ignore. When studying air, children should compare their experiences to the investigations they have done with solids and liquids. Using consistent dialogue can help children extend crosscutting concepts:

Sample Next Generation Science Standards

Disciplinary Core Idea

PS1.A: Structure and Properties of Matter

Different properties are suited to different purposes. (2-PS1-2, 2-PS1-3)

Performance Expectation

Students who demonstrate understanding can:

Plan and conduct an investigation to describe and classify different kinds of materials by their observable properties. (2-PS1-1)

(NGSS Lead States 2013)

- Solids have a definite **shape** and definite **size** (volume).

- Liquids have a definite size (volume) but take any shape.

- Gas (air) doesn't have any definite size or shape.

- All matter (solids, liquids, and gases) has **weight**.

- All matter (solids, liquids, and gases) can push (exert force).

- We can use our senses to study the properties of matter.

This unit includes comparison of a variety of kinds of bubbles and other materials that contain gas. Bubbles are thin layers of liquid containing a gas. The more cohesive the liquid is, the longer the bubble will maintain its shape.

Like gravity and friction, these concepts will only be partially understood at the early childhood level. But the exciting explorations you can do are great stimuli for developing language and imagination.

Sample Common Core Standards

Use words and phrases acquired through conversations, reading and being read to, and responding to texts, including using adjectives and adverbs to describe. (CCSS Language Arts L.2.6) (CCSS Initiative 2016a, 27)

Directly compare two objects with a measurable attribute in common, to see which object has "more of"/"less of" the attribute, and describe the difference. (CCSS.Math.K.MD.A.2) (CCSS Initiative 2016b, 12)

Engineering Challenge

Ask children to compare paper airplanes, ideally with older partners. As children mature in their ability to construct the airplanes and measure their flight, they can experiment with different variables: thickness of paper, small weights (like paper clips or sticky dots) on the wings or body of the plane, small slits in the wings.

Safety Note

Space is the most significant factor in safety when you're working with a group of children. When we bring more children (such as peer helpers) into a room, we make it more crowded and make accidents more likely to occur. This activity, like many others, is best done in a big space such as a gym or cafeteria, or outdoors.

Templates for airplanes and gliders are available at this NASA website (www.grc.nasa.gov/www/k-12/Summer_Training/Elementary97/dart.html), as well as at the websites in appendix B. The simplest NASA template, the "dart," is reproduced on page 113.

The simplest airplane contest is one of distance, of course. But the ability to fly straight is another way to measure the performance of paper planes. Little hands may be less able to launch the planes in a straight direction. This is another situation in which peers' help is both useful and fun.

Paper Airplanes

by Janet Wong

Each team in our class has twenty minutes
to make a paper plane that can fly the farthest.

One sheet of paper per plane.
No other stuff.
Five pieces of paper per team for models.
Each team works in a separate area. No spies.

We brainstorm.
Short and wide or long and thin?
Wing tips up or down or flat?
Pointed nose or squared off?

We make five models and test them all.
With one minute to choose our favorite,
our best plane flies straight into a wall

on its third test flight at the very same time
that our principal walks through the hallway
and steps on it. *Crunch!*

It is broken beyond repair.
Glenn crumples it into a ball and throws it.
It goes farther than anything else we made.
We have ten seconds left when—*ding dong!*—

a question pops into our minds.
A stupid question?
Maybe. But we run to ask our teacher anyway:
Does it have to look like a regular plane?

Kids laugh when they see our ball-plane.
But no one laughs when we jump and shout:
We won! We won!! We won!!!

Try It!

Many living things use the air to help them move. Birds and bees fly. Some squirrels can glide. So can many kinds of seeds, like those of the maple tree. Some people call this part of the maple a "helicopter." The real name is "samara," named for a Japanese sword.

You can make a paper helicopter that falls like a maple seed. Fold a paper like this and put a paper clip on it.

Hold your helicopter as high as you can and drop it.

How does it fall? _____

_____

How far does it fall? _____

_____

Paper clip →

Now make a better helicopter. You can make it heavier or lighter, or make small cuts in the blades.

What did you do to make the helicopter fly better?

_____

_____

Have a helicopter race.

Draw a picture of the helicopter that flew the best:

Dear Families:

The matter around us can be solid, liquid, or gas. This week we are studying **air**, a gas. Of course, most of the time we cannot see it. But we feel the effects of air all the time—warm or cool, windy or calm, dry or moist.

Children can use their senses to discover things about air, using the same ideas they use to look at liquids. You can help by using old and new vocabulary as you encourage children to be more observant.

In our STEM lessons, we always try to make connections. When children use the same skills and vocabulary in different settings, they develop deeper understanding. We use the words "push" and "pull" all the time as we study science. You can help by using these words for air, too! If there is a wind, you might ask, "I wonder what's pushing it?" (Actually, it's the sun and its warmth.) If the room is too hot and you want to use a fan, you can use the same sort of conversation, saying, "Let's push some air around."

In a car, you might (safely) explore how air might pull a feather or tiny scrap of paper out of an open window. The air that goes through your vacuum pulls dust and dirt into the machine. Your hair dryer pushes air around to help dry your hair, and the hand dryer in a public restroom both heats and pushes air against your hands.

We are making small paper helicopters to see how they fly. Try them at home. All you need is paper and paper clips.

Whenever children investigate on their own, they develop questions. Some of those questions you may want to explore at home. But it is always terrific when children bring their questions to school. If a good question comes up, send it along.

Thanks for being great STEM partners. And have fun.

Be an Engineer!

Can you make an airplane out of paper? Here's a plan from NASA. Start with a square piece of paper. Fold it where the line is dotted, like this:

How far can your plane fly?

_____

_____

_____

_____

Now change the plane. Take a paper clip or dot sticker and make one part heavier.

Did it fly farther?

_____

_____

_____

_____

(Remember, a test must be fair!)

How to make a Dart Airplane

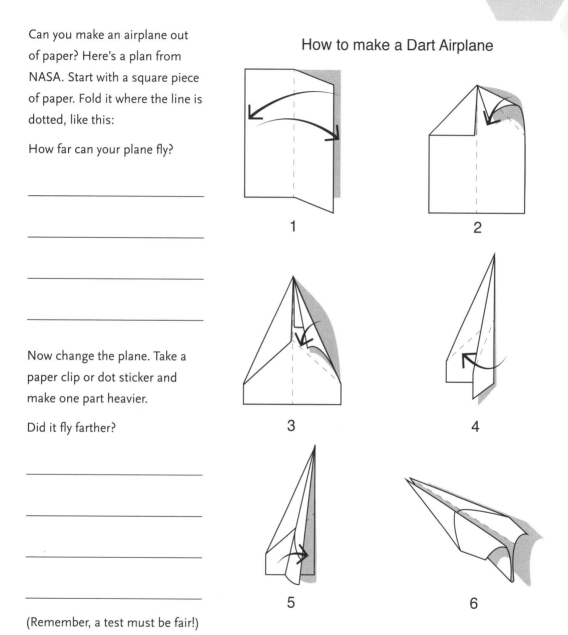

1

2

3

4

5

6

Leonardo da Vinci: STEM Star

Leonardo da Vinci loved to do many things.

He was an artist. He loved to draw.

Leonardo was a painter, too.

He invented new kinds of paints, made of things like egg and oil. Some of his paints were beautiful. Some didn't last very long.

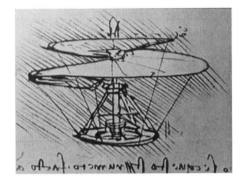

Leonardo invented weapons for kings. He once made a metal statue, then melted it to make a cannon.

He drew inventions that were like helicopters, bicycles, and even an airplane that flew like a bat.

But most of his ideas were never built.

What do you like to do? _____

_____

Do you have more than one talent? _____

_____

Do you have a good idea? _____

_____

What could you invent? _____

_____

_____

Sun and Shadow

The Big Question: What Can We Learn from the Light of the Sun?

Creating Context

Sunlight is all around us. It warms us and provides **energy**. Our eyes can see a part of the energy of sunlight. Our senses (skin) can feel its heat. But like many phenomena, sun energy can be taken for granted. With care, children can make many observations about sunlight and can make predictions, arguments, and conclusions about these observations.

The light, heat, and colors of the sun's rays are all appropriate topics for early childhood investigation. They can be seen and measured without moving into astronomy. This unit begins with light and shadow, the most direct and developmentally appropriate phenomena to investigate. Extensions allow children to explore spectra and rainbows.

The explorations of light and shadow outdoors can become the basis for planning a garden, the final engineering challenge of this book, in unit 12. So it is worth a little extra time to collect the data.

Safety Note

Students should never look at the sun and should always be cautious about overexposing their skin. This group of activities looks at the effect of visible light on the surface of the earth. The sun is pleasant and warm but can harm your skin and eyes. Discuss the value of sunglasses and sunscreen. Visit the Sunwise website for more information: www.neefusa.org/sunwise.

Engage

Lawrence F. Lowery's book *I Wonder Why? Dark as a Shadow* introduces different scenarios of shadows and places to readers. Begin by sharing small sections with the class. Then make shadows.

You can get a shadow anytime of the day or night as long as you have a light source, something to block the light source, and a place for the shadow to fall. You can open just one window in the room to make a directed source of light or use flashlights in a darker room.

Sample Next Generation Science Standards

Disciplinary Core Idea

Sunlight warms Earth's surface. (K-PS3-2)

Performance Expectations

Students who demonstrate understanding can:

Make observations to determine the effect of sunlight on Earth's surface. (K-PS3-1)

Plan and conduct investigations to determine the effects of placing objects made with different materials in the path of a beam of light. (1-PS4-3)

(NGSS Lead States 2013)

Children will want to recreate the shadows in their own way. This is an excellent opportunity for shadow play. Create a shadow drama in which children act out a simple story. Or set up a guessing game in which children look at shadows projected on the wall and guess what they are.

Then take a shadow walk. Walk indoors and out to see where shadows are most visible. On a warm day, place ice cubes in sun and shadow, and return to them a few minutes later to see which ones melted quicker.

Explore

Materials can be transparent (see-through), translucent (partially see-through), or opaque (blocking all light). Have children select materials of various types from a collection to see if they can create shadows, then classify them. For example, shining a flashlight through translucent plastic, a sieve, or mesh material won't make a shadow. A toy or cardboard cutout can block light.

Then integrate shadow making with mathematics. Ask children to select and name various shapes for shadow play: triangles, squares, rectangles, and circles. Challenge children to identify the shape (circle, rectangle, triangle) from the light that is cast by the flashlight. Create characters that are combinations of shapes and use them for the shadow play.

Explain

For shadows to be created, there must be a source of light, something to block that light, and a surface for the shadow to fall on. Light travels fast and in straight lines unless it is bent by something like a mirror, water, or thick glass. That's why we can make cutouts of various shapes and create a shadow play;

this can show that light is going in a straight line. Shadows are created when something blocks the light, because light cannot go around the object.

Elaborate

The sun's **energy** warms us. The experience of comparing melting ice cubes on a walk can begin helping children understand heat.

Give children plastic thermometers to place on top of an outdoor table and underneath it. Ask the children to predict which area will be cooler, and then test their predictions. Then use ice cubes again to check out those predictions. See where cubes melt most quickly.

Shadows can be used to tell the time of day. Create a sundial with any stick in a place outdoors without shade. Use a hula hoop to create a standard circle around the stick. The central point (gnomon) will cast different shadows at different times of the day. Allow children to go outside and record where the shadows fall at various times of the day. Don't do it just for a single day, but for several sunny days in a row.

Evaluate

Sunlight-reactive beads, available from many science supply stores and from Sunwise (www.neefusa.org/sunwise), can be used to test predictions about sun and shadow. Many of the sunlight-reactive beads fit easily on thin coffee stir sticks or pipe cleaners, so they can be easily managed by young hands. Allow children to place a strand of five beads in a place they predict will be sunny and another in a place they predict will be shady. After ten minutes, compare the colors of the beads. Evaluate with the routine of claim, evidence, and reasoning, or "What do you predict? What did you find? Why did that happen?" As children grow in logical skills, their explanations come closer to their data and follow more logically from their predictions.

Content Background

Light and heat are both forms of electromagnetic **energy**. So are radio waves and microwaves. Each has a different wavelength.

The rays of the sun travel in waves, and the waves travel in straight lines. They can pass through transparent (see-through) materials, partially pass through translucent (partially see-through) materials, and be blocked by opaque materials that we cannot see through.

We perceive visible light as white, but it's really a mixture of different wavelengths (colors), and the spectrum is really a blend of colors. We sometimes identify these colors as red, orange, yellow, green, blue, indigo, and violet. (There are no separate colors involved; this is just a convenience for our imagination.) Because some wavelengths pass through some materials (like prisms and water mist) at different speeds, they separate and form rainbows. They also separate a bit as the earth rotates and the sun's rays pass through the atmosphere at an angle, causing beautiful sunrises and sunsets.

The wavelengths of electromagnetic energy can change as they encounter different materials, too. For example, when visible light hits lighter-colored materials, it may reflect or bounce off them, but when it hits very dark materials, the wavelength may move to the infrared range—and become heat. That's why white clothes feel cooler than dark clothes, and homes with lighter roofs need less air-conditioning.

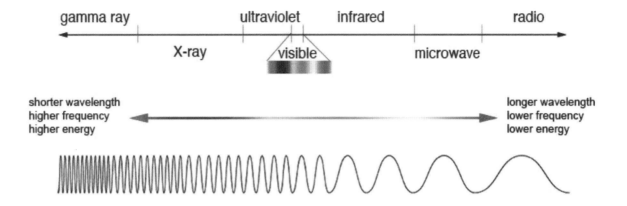

Integrate

Lawrence Lowery's book *I Wonder Why? Dark as a Shadow* can provide a good beginning for explorations of light and shadow. He also offers simple explanations about light in a format that answers some questions and is bound to generate more questions in *I Wonder Why? Light and Color*.

More Literature to Integrate

A perfect time to study shadows is in February. February 2 is Groundhog Day. On this day, according to tradition, the famous groundhog Punxsutawney Phil provides the forecast for whether spring is around the corner. If Phil sees his shadow and returns to his home in the ground, there will be six more weeks of winter. If Phil does not see his shadow, spring will arrive early. This tradition has been going on since 1887 in the town of Punxsutawney, Pennsylvania.

Read the book *Groundhog's Dilemma* by Kristen Remenar to find out how the groundhog solves his dilemma on Groundhog Day.

Engineering Challenge

Children can use sunlight-reactive beads to find out where there is sun and shade in the neighborhood. Children can also use the beads to test sunscreens.

 EARLY EXPLORERS

Pair each young explorer with an older peer. Challenge the children to catch their shadows. The pairs of children might explore the playground or an indoor place with lots of directed window light for the best place to make shadows. The older peer can trace the shadows with sidewalk chalk. Ask children to do a shadow dance and make their own shadow move.

Try It!

Draw your shadow!

Morning	Noon	Afternoon

Explain to your friend why your shadow changed: _____

_____

_____

_____

_____

_____

_____

Be an Engineer!

Be a chemical engineer. Look at how sunscreen works. Use your sun beads. Put some sunscreen on some beads and not on others. Put both groups of beads in the sun. How do you know that the sun has hit the beads?

No Sunscreen	Weak Sunscreen	Strong Sunscreen

Then walk around outdoors on a sunny day. Put beads in places that are very sunny and places that are shady. Use a map to mark the sunny spots.

Build a sundial. Because the sun's shadows change each hour of the day, we can use them to tell the time of day. Look at the picture of a sundial here. Think about what you might use to make the same thing.

Mark the first shadow early in the day. Ask a friend to predict where the shadow will be the next hour. Was the prediction correct?_____

Watch the shadows each hour for a day, and mark where they fall. (You can use flags, tape, or sidewalk chalk.) Do it again the next day. Did the shadows change? _____

Dear Families:

This week we are studying sun and shadows. We will be making shadow puppets and following how our shadows change from morning to afternoon. This is an easy activity to replicate on a sunny day.

The word "**energy**" continues to be an important one. We've talked about the energy needed for pushes and pulls, and the energy that changes solids to liquids. Now we will look at light energy (which can, of course, change to heat energy). Humans have energy, too—starting with the sun energy that is stored in our foods, keeping us warm and active. There are lots of opportunities to reinforce both the concept and the key vocabulary.

In our activities, we'll remind children to protect their eyes from the sun. They should never look at the sun or very bright lights. You can help us by repeating these warnings at home.

We'll also be reminding children to use sunscreen, to reinforce the idea that the sun's rays can be dangerous if we don't protect ourselves. When your children go outside, remind them to use appropriate protection, including hats, shirts, and sunscreen.

Thanks for being great STEM partners. And have fun.

Franz Greiter: STEM Star

Franz Greiter loved to climb mountains. At the top of a mountain, the sun is very bright.

Franz often got sunburned. Sunburn can make you very ill. It is important to prevent sunburn.

Franz went to school.

He became a chemical engineer.

He mixed chemicals and tested them. Some of the mixtures helped keep the sun from burning skin.

Some people climb mountains.

Some people play ball.

What do you do outside? _____

_____

_____

When do you need sunscreen? _____

_____

_____

What could you tell a friend who is going to the beach? _____

_____

Hot Stuff, Cool Science

The Big Question: How Do Objects Get Warmer or Cooler?

Creating Context

Energy is invisible, but its effects are easy to observe. In previous units, children explored how energy can make things change. They also explored how energy (in the form of heat) could pass through different materials (like air), and could be blocked by other materials (like gloves or insulation). In unit 9, children explored the sun's energy. In this unit, they explore how energy makes a material warmer or cooler. The crosscutting concept of energy continues to be a key. Continue to use the term "energy" as often as you can. In the engineering challenge, children will look at another crosscutting concept, structure and function, as it relates to energy transfer.

Engage

Take two identical toys (ideally, toys with personality) that are light and dark in color. Put one under a lamp. Then ask children to feel each toy, describing it with the word "warm" or "cool." The darker character will be a bit warmer. Allow children to make up a dialogue for the characters. Use a forehead tape–style children's thermometer to measure temperature. Temperature guns (infrared thermometers) are available at hardware stores for minimal cost; these can also be used for this activity. Whenever you introduce a new technology like this with young children, it is helpful to compare the results with physical sensations and simpler measuring instruments. For example, when you're comparing two identical objects in sun and shade, first feel them, then use temperature tape, then, if you choose, use the temperature gun.

 TEACHER TIP

Today's children don't have much experience with traditional thermometers, and it takes some explaining to compare the results of the sort of temperature-taking device they know to what a scientist uses. Collecting a variety of temperature-measuring devices and allowing children to experiment with them is a useful activity. Used forehead tape, plastic school thermometers, cooking and refrigerator thermometers, and (optionally) a battery-powered temperature probe (sold at hardware stores).

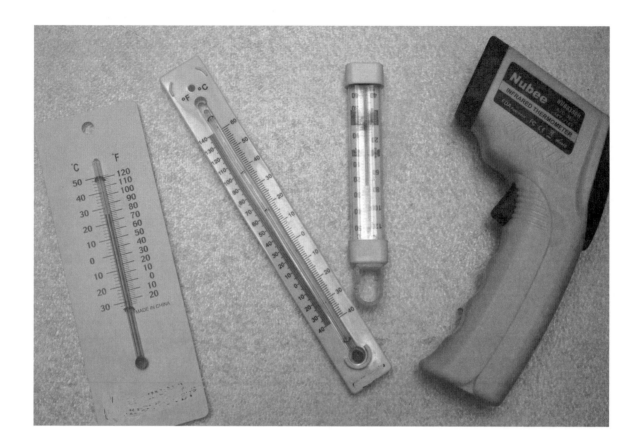

Explore

Wander around your environment. Find places where it is warmer (perhaps the kitchen or cafeteria) and places where it is cooler (maybe a drafty hallway or door). On a map of the building, color warmer areas with a warm color (red or orange) and cooler areas with a cool color (blue or green).

 TEACHER TIP

The Land of Bump (https://lob.concord.org), a website from Concord Consortium, is an online simulation of the movement of energy in invisible particles. Despite the fact that the level of simulation is above what most consider developmentally appropriate in the early years, there is strong empirical evidence that this technology is useful to stimulate great discussions among children. See also Concord Consortium's related teacher resources, including videos, at https://concord.org/stem-resources.

Explain

The **energy** that makes things warm us can come from the sun, from the fuel that powers heaters and other human-made machines, and even from the food that powers our own bodies. We can feel warmth with our senses. Energy like heat moves from areas where it is high (warmer) to areas where it is low (cooler.) So a very warm cookie soon gets cool because the heat energy moves away and spreads out, and a Popsicle melts because energy in the air makes it warmer. Review with children their other experiences about movement of heat energy, such as when they compared gloves and tried to build an insulator for a soda can.

Elaborate

Keeping warm or cool is an important safety factor for children. Show the classic *Sesame Street* video of Kermit and Grover titled "Hot and Cold" (www.youtube.com/watch?v=cqXSinx4-aU). Stop the video just after the one-minute mark, and ask students to respond to Grover's question "How can I get warm?"

Using magazines, catalogs, or a collection of online photos, ask children to identify ways of keeping warm or cool. Classify them in a personal or group display.

Ask children what it means to sweat. (When water evaporates from our skin, it uses the heat **energy** from our hot body, taking away that heat and cooling us down.) Then discuss the temperature needs of pets. Dogs have a higher normal body temperature and have no sweat glands. They cool down through panting, but they can become very ill very quickly in a hot environment like a car. Ask children to verbalize how to keep pets and people safe in warm temperatures.

Evaluate

Begin a story about a very warm or very cold day. Ask children to complete (orally or by acting out) the ideas about keeping warm or cool.

 EARLY EXPLORERS

Post a character on the board, and provide overlays of appropriate clothing to choose for each day's weather. Ask children to act out how it feels to be cold or hot. Then ask them to choose from a pile of clothing those that fit their condition. Vary your dress-up area to accommodate weather conditions.

Children may remember the ice cream or snow character that melted in unit 6. Do this activity again, and ask, "Could we keep the character from melting if we put some clothing on it?" Try any wrapping (bubble wrap or plastic wrap works) and compare.

Sample Next Generation Science Standards

Disciplinary Core Ideas

PS1.A: Structure and Properties of Matter

- Different kinds of matter exist and many of them can be either solid or liquid, depending on temperature. Matter can be described and classified by its observable properties. (2-PS1-1)
- Different properties are suited to different purposes. (2-PS1-2, 2-PS1-3)

Performance Expectations

Students who demonstrate understanding can:

- Plan and conduct an investigation to describe and classify different kinds of materials by their observable properties. (2-PS1-1)
- Analyze data obtained from testing different materials to determine which materials have the properties that are best for an intended solution. (2-PS1-2)

(NGSS Lead States 2013)

Safety Note

Incandescent lightbulbs can shatter and can get very hot. Make sure the light you use is shielded and that students do not go near it. LED lights do not get as hot but are still breakable glass.

Old-fashioned thermometers made of glass can break easily. Use thermometers with metal or plastic backing for safety.

Engineering Challenge

In two previous units, children explored the idea of insulation. In this unit, they continue to explore insulation by building a house and developing various solutions to keep it cool. For simplicity, younger children may simply change the material on the roof of a "house" made from a box. You can precut small boxes with one small window and one small door. Provide a number of materials for the roof, and allow children to choose. These might include paper, cloth, plastic "grassy" mat material, carpet squares, rubber, or bubble wrap. (Add your list of needs to your family letter to get more participation.) Use an incandescent lamp to warm the houses, or put them in a sunny window. You can also just change the colors of the roofs and compare temperature changes that way.

Measure the change in temperature over time. Large bar graphs are the most graphic way to help children compare their observations.

Content Background

Light and heat are both forms of electromagnetic **energy**. Heat is produced by infrared rays. Certain materials can change the wavelengths of the energy that hits them. For example, dark materials on the surface of the earth change visible light to heat. Energy can't be created or destroyed, but it can be changed and spread out so it is less effective in some specific range.

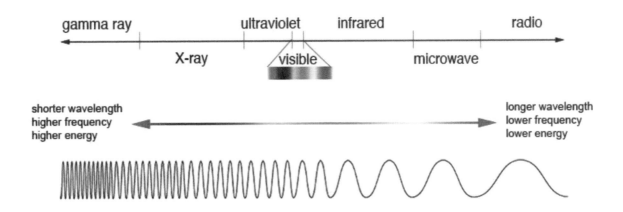

Shining a light on any surface is likely to warm it up, but the effects are different depending on the color and nature of the materials. Dark colors absorb almost all wavelengths of visible light. Most wavelengths bounce off a white surface.

When a person (whose normal body temperature is around 98.6°F) touches an object made of metal, the metal conducts heat from the fingers to the object more quickly than if that same hand were touching wood or plastic. So the metal feels cooler, even though it might be the same temperature as the wood or plastic.

Even though we would not assess for understanding at this level, it is important to watch our own vocabulary. Heat is energy, and temperature is the effect of that energy on matter.

Integrate

Emily Morgan's *Next Time You See a Sunset* models the sort of dialogue that might take place between a teacher, parent, or caregiver and an observant child. Morgan explains the reasons for the spectacular colors and shadows that accompany sunrise and sunset. If you can, share

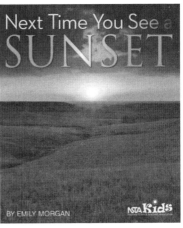

a few pages with families to help them increase their dialogue with their children. Use this model to explain to children that many kinds of energy come from the sun. We see colors (and can see them better with a prism), but we also receive heat.

More Literature to Integrate

Paul A. Reynolds's book *Sydney and Simon: Full Steam Ahead!* includes many examples of heat and energy that can be discussed and repeated.

Lawrence Lowery's *I Wonder Why? Light and Color* extends the explanation that teachers may have begun reading in *Next Time You See a Sunset*.

In this and the next chapter, students look at the structural integrity of buildings. Any story of the Three Little Pigs works well. We particularly enjoy John Scieszka's *The True Story of the Three Little Pigs*.

Be an Engineer!

Building Your House

Let's build a house! We want to make it cool in the summer.

Choose a material for the roof. Explain to a friend why you like that material.

What color should you make your roof? Explain to a friend why you like that color.

Predict which house will stay cool:

Testing Your House

Put a thermometer in your house.

Put your house in the sun.

Did your design keep your house cool? _____

_____

_____

_____

How do you know? _____

_____

_____

Improving Your House

How would you make your house better? _____

_____

Dear Families:

We are looking forward to another *energetic* week of STEM explorations. Light and heat are forms of **energy**. We are looking at how light energy can change to heat energy. When sunlight hits dark objects on the surface of the earth, much of it changes to heat energy. Light bounces off lighter colors more easily.

This week we are testing materials that might be on the roofs of houses to keep people warm in the winter and cool in the summer. Can you take a walk or drive with your child and compare roofs? Are some light and some dark? Can students see shingles, tiles, or tar? Of course not all roofs are visible from the ground, but many are.

We'll be exploring more insulation activities. In previous units, we tested gloves to see if they could keep our hands warm, and we tested an insulation material for a soda can. We could use some scrap materials for our experiments. If you have small squares of carpet or grass mats, an old rubber car mat, bubble wrap or thick cloth, we could use these items as roofing materials for our experimental houses. We'll change the roofs of our model houses, put them in a warm, lighted area, and see which roof works best.

We will read about architect Frank Lloyd Wright, who not only made beautiful homes but also made them safer. Ask your child for ideas to make your home safer.

Thanks for being great STEM partners. And have fun!

Frank Lloyd Wright: STEM Star

Young Frank Lloyd Wright loved to be outside. His mother was a teacher. His father was a musician.

He drew trees, hills, and outside places.

In school he became an architect.

He had to study drawing, science, math, and engineering.

When an architect builds something, all of these are important!

Most architects design big buildings. Frank wanted to build houses for people. He wanted the houses to be as beautiful as nature.

What parts of nature could you use to make your house nicer? _____

_____

_____

Frank also built safer homes and hotels in places where there are earthquakes.

What could make your home safer? _____

_____

_____

_____

Wind and Water

The Big Question: How Do Wind and Water Change the Shape of the Land?

Creating Context

The transition from physical science to earth science is an easy one. In many ways, earth science is simply the application of physical science to the world around us. This unit continues to talk about energy from the sun and explores how sun-powered **wind** and **water** change the shape of the land.

Engage

Take walks outdoors to look for landforms that children might know. Are there hills? Natural swales? Human-made ditches and berms? Streams?

Find an area where the soil is eroded. This can be near a ditch, at the edge of asphalt, or under a piece of playground equipment. Ask children where the

Sample Next Generation Science Standards

Disciplinary Core Idea

ESS2.A: Earth Materials and Systems

Wind and water can change the shape of the land. (2-ESS2-1)

Performance Expectation

Students who demonstrate understanding can:

Compare multiple solutions designed to slow or prevent wind or water from changing the shape of the land. (2-ESS2-1)

(NGSS Lead States 2013)

soil went, and what force caused it to disappear. (Children may be able to suggest **wind** or **water**, but might often suggest that human action was the cause.) Ask them what would happen if the process continued.

◉◉ EARLY EXPLORERS

If you have a hill or low area nearby, take children for a walk outdoors to experience landforms themselves. Encourage children to talk about how they are traveling: "We are going up now. We are going down now." Then provide clay or playdough in the classroom for children to create a model area with hills, valleys, ditches, or swales—anything that is familiar to them. Small human characters can populate this model, and children can describe what the characters would say. Relating a model like this to the real world will be a big step for early explorers, but telling stories about characters can help them begin.

Explore

Using a sand table or disposable paint pans filled with sterile soil or sand, create a slope. Small sprigs of plants can be added to make it more realistic. Blow on the soil through straws to make "**wind**." "Rain" on the soil by pouring **water** from a plastic cup with holes in the bottom. Ask children to describe in words and pictures how the soil changes as air or water flows on it. Then compare soil samples with sand. Does the wind move the fine soil particles differently than it moves the bigger sand particles? Provide plastic hand lenses so that children can observe and draw the particles. Finally, ask children to predict whether their same actions with "wind" and "rain" could move aquarium gravel, and then try it. Safety tip: This must be done gently. Eye protection is appropriate.

Explain

Children have learned that the forces of **wind** and **water** can change the shape of landforms by pushing. Wind and water sometimes act together to make even greater changes. We can model how wind or water moves earth materials. Some particles are bigger and some are smaller. Lighter particles might move with a little wind or slow water. Heavy particles need more push to make them move.

Elaborate

Using photos, show children areas that have been eroded by **wind** and **water**. These photos should be appropriate to the location in which the children live—desert, beach, a roadside area where clearing has occurred, or a hill. Encourage them to think of things that can be done to prevent erosion. If you have a construction site nearby with small plastic barriers to erosion, point them out.

Evaluate

Using photos, ask children to identify what force changed the land—**wind**, **water**, or living things. Photos may show combinations of forces. (For example, waves are wind and water.) Look for arguing with evidence—expressing an idea and giving a reason—rather than content knowledge.

Depending on the age of the children, there are several ways to measure erosion. The youngest environmental engineers might just photograph or draw the hills they create. The pans can also be placed on larger trays (such as rectangular cookie sheets), and the soil that overflows with the water can be observed and measured that way. For older children or more extended investigations, the soil that remains can be allowed to dry and then can be weighed.

Sample Common Core Standards

Participate in collaborative conversations with diverse partners about *kindergarten topics and texts* with peers and adults in small and larger groups. (CCSS. ELA-Literacy.SL.K.1) (CCSS Initiative 2016a, 23)

Measure and estimate liquid volumes and masses of objects using standard units of grams (g), kilograms (kg), and liters (l). Add, subtract, multiply, or divide to solve one-step word problems involving masses or volumes that are given in the same units, e.g., by using drawings (such as a beaker with a measurement scale) to represent the problem. (CCSS. Math.Content.3.MD.A.2) (CCSS Initiative 2016b, 25)

Integrate

Sarah C. Campbell's *Mysterious Patterns: Finding Fractals in Nature* includes an example of an alluvial (river-made) pattern. There are many other examples of fractals in the book. Children can quickly learn to find these in their neighborhood. They won't see them as fractals, but as interesting shapes. Creating a similar pattern by dropping water on soil or sand can build a foundation for later learning.

More Literature to Integrate

- Both the website and related award-winning publications by "Dirtmeister" Steve Tomecek are very valuable resources for young children. *Dirtmeister's Nitty Gritty Planet Earth* offers a rich array of materials to use as children explore earth materials. Each chapter begins with a child's question. After sharing one of the questions and the answers, ask students to generate their own.

- Ellen Lawrence's book *FUNdamental Experiments: Dirt* includes many very simple activities that you can do with dirt.

Engineering Challenge

Wind and **water** push and pull the surface of the earth around. Landforms are changed by these pushes and pulls. In the engineering challenge that follows, children look at how soil or sand on the earth's surface can be protected by using plants, rock levees, or other structures children can imagine or design. The activity can be as simple or as extended as you'd like. If the houses from unit 10 are small, they can be placed at the top of the surface to see if they stay put.

Content Background

Most of the changes we see on the surface of the earth are moved by energy from the sun. Earth is also moved by internal energy (mostly radioactive) and is a tectonic planet, but that would not be an observation that young children could see, feel, or touch in any normal circumstance.

In addition to water, earth materials include rocks, minerals, and soil. Some materials are classified by their chemical composition. For example, clay is aluminum silicate. Limestone is calcium carbonate. Other materials are classified by particle size. Sand might be from 0.01 to 0.07 inch in size; it could be made of silicon dioxide (like quartz or glass) or limestone, or it could be bits of shell, coral, or volcanic ash. Bigger particles might be called cobble or gravel.

Soil is a composite of minerals, plant and animal materials, gases, and living things. Without that mix, it could not easily hold the water and air needed to sustain living things.

Be an Engineer!

Some people live at the bottom of a hill. It is always muddy there.

Design a better hill.

Use a model of sand and soil. Put materials in it that will stop the mud.

Then use a cup with water to test what happens in the rain.

Record an ad to help people understand how to save their soil.

Try It!

This is a picture of Alaska. It was taken from an airplane.

What could have made these tracks?

_____

_____

_____

_____

_____

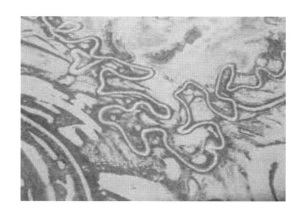

Go to a place that has sand or soil.

Use a straw. Push the sand or soil with "wind" from your straw. Can you make the same pattern?

Get a cup with small holes in the bottom.

Can you make the pattern by letting water fall on the sand or soil?

Dear Families:

This week our class is learning how forces in nature—like **wind** and **water**—can change the shape of the land. Illustrations of this are all around us.

Take a walk or a ride. Ask children to observe hills, ditches, valleys, or even carefully planted lawns. Ask them to describe the land. Words like "flat," "muddy," "sandy," or "rocky" are all appropriate. And the words we used in other STEM adventures, like "push," "pull," "warm," "cool," "heavy," and "light," are also appropriate. Any observations are good ones.

Then go on a scavenger hunt. Find a place where wind or water changed the area. This might be a little ditch, a pile of sand near a building, a puddle, or a pond. If you have access to a camera, grab a photo for our class discussion. If not, paper and crayons might provide the picture.

Like all of our lessons in science, we try to make connections. We've talked a lot about pushes, pulls, **wind** and **water**, warm and cold, and energy. All of these ideas apply to the way that land is shaped in nature.

When children observe nature, they often come up with questions of their own. If you have an answer, great! But that's not necessary. You can investigate together with your child, or write a note together to bring to class. We'll collect children's questions for future investigations.

Every yard and every neighborhood offers science lessons.

Thanks for sharing yours with us. You are great STEM partners. Have fun.

Joseph Lazaro: STEM Star

Beaches are special places. Waves and wind change beaches every day.

Each time you visit, the beach is different.

Sand can move. It could be erosion. Erosion is when the water washes away the sand.

Plants can hold the sand. But plants can grow or die.

Protecting beaches is important for the plants, the animals, and the people who live near the beaches.

Joseph Lazaro lives near the ocean in Louisiana.
He was worried about beach erosion.

Do you know how big a football field is? In Louisiana that much sand disappears every day!

Joseph invented a way to slow down erosion.

His invention used a strip of plastic in the water just beyond the beach. The plastic strip slowed the waves. The sand stayed on the beach.

Growing Engineers

The Big Question: How Can We Use the Sun's Energy on Earth?

Creating Context

In previous units, children have studied **energy** in a number of ways. This is what *Framework* calls a crosscutting concept. Children have looked at pushes and pulls, including the pull of gravity and the pushback of friction; the effect of energy on matter (solid to liquid); and the energy of sun and wind on natural and human-made structures. Now they apply these understandings to living things through a garden. This is a great time to involve the entire learning community in a project that forms a summative assessment and a source of pride.

Engage

With photos (for younger children) or a map (for older children) of your program's yard, review the observations of areas of light and shade from unit 9 and wind and rain from unit 11. These may include photos or maps of sunlight, and data from pinwheels or wind socks and rain gauges in several areas that might be candidates for a garden. Collect more data where appropriate. Display these data for discussion.

 TEACHER TIP

As in unit 9, children can measure sunlight by looking at shadows (no shadow, fuzzy shadow, clear shadow). Be fair and measure shadows at the same time each day.

A rain gauge can be as simple as two dose cups, available from many medical suppliers or from a nursing home (sterilize before children handle). Put a glob of nontoxic rubber cement under one cup to provide a base, then pop a second cup inside. Then you can remove the inner cup each day, record the amount of rainwater in it, and replace it.

Pinwheels can provide rough measures of wind (still, slow, fast). A wind sock can be compared to photos (droopy, partially extended, completely extended) to make a graph, or photos can be taken and recorded on a class calendar or chart.

Finding a place for your garden might be hard. Some buildings are built on areas where the soil has not been tested. If there is any possibility that soil would not be suitable for gardening, or if there is a danger of another sort, consider gardening in pots or hanging gardens.

Sample Next Generation Science Standards

Disciplinary Core Idea

LS2.A: Interdependent Relationships in Ecosystems

Plants depend on water and light to grow. (2-LS2-1)

Performance Expectation

Students who demonstrate understanding can:

Plan and conduct an investigation to determine if plants need sunlight and water to grow. (2-LS2-1)

ETS1: Engineering Design

Develop a simple sketch, drawing, or physical model to illustrate how the shape of an object helps it function as needed to solve a given problem. (K-2-ETS1-2)

(NGSS Lead States 2013)

EARLY EXPLORERS

For the youngest explorers, several pepper or bean seeds in a plastic bag (with a wet paper towel) make a good start for a garden. When they germinate, potting soil in a paper cup can become a home for the plants. Allow children to choose the right size cup to measure the water they will give their plants each day—not too big, not too small. Ask, "Is your seed growing? How do you know? Are you growing? How do you know?"

When it's time to move the plants outdoors, choosing and using tools provide good lessons. Collect plastic tools like hand spades and claw rakes. Ask, "Which one is best for planting? Which one is best for loosening soil around the plants?"

Explore

What is a garden? What kinds of things can grow in a garden? Ask children to interview the person who cooks food in your program to determine what sorts of foods the cook could use that might be grown in a program garden. Depending on your geographic location, the possibilities will vary widely. Simple pot gardens with herbs, cherry tomatoes, and peppers can be pizza gardens. Programs with larger grounds and perhaps a group of family helpers might attempt something more expansive.

Divide children into groups and ask them to come up with their own ideas for a garden. Then use a chart like the one on page 147 ("My Garden Engineering Project") to help them decide whether the plants they want would be practical for their garden. (This chart is partially complete. Children should add their own ideas and use text or Internet sources to fill out the rest.)

Explain

Ask a panel of adults in your learning community to help select the best garden plan. Children should argue from evidence (in the terms of the *Framework*) to sell their idea to the panel. (Don't make this a competition where there are winners or losers. This series of presentations should be a way of getting good advice!)

Elaborate

With a calendar, plan out the garden schedule. Will it be warm enough for the plants to grow? Will the plants grow when children aren't around to water them? If so, can families take responsibility for weeding, watering, and harvesting?

Evaluate

The time commitment to a school garden isn't normally practical for a summative assessment, but each week can be a celebration. In the sort of journal described in Steve Rich's book *My School Yard Garden*, ask children to rate the progress of the project. A rubric might look like this:

My Garden Engineering Project			
Observations	❏ None	❏ Some	❏ Many
Planning	❏ None	❏ Some	❏ Many
Advice	❏ None	❏ Some	❏ Many
Design	❏ None	❏ A little	❏ A lot
Redesign	❏ None	❏ A little	❏ A lot

Children often have a difficult time imagining how big their plants will be when they have grown. Use lids from kitchen pans to mark out the space a small plant might need. For example, a tomato or pepper plant might need the circular space of a twelve-inch frying pan lid. A squash might need the space of a hula hoop!

Sample Common Core Standards

Participate in collaborative conversations with diverse partners about *kindergarten topics and texts* with peers and adults in small and larger groups. (CCSS. ELA-Literacy.SL.K.1) (CCSS Initiative 2016a, 23)

Estimate lengths using units of inches, feet, centimeters, and meters. (CCSS.Math. Content.2.MD.A.3) (CCSS Initiative 2016b, 20)

Integrate

Steve Rich's book *My School Yard Garden* illustrates not only the engineering process of designing a garden but also the value of journaling as a project happens.

More Literature to Integrate

- Arden Bucklin-Sporer and Rachel Kathleen Pringle offer another guide in their book *How to Grow a School Garden*.

- Sarah C. Campbell's books *Mysterious Patterns: Finding Fractals in Nature* and *Growing Patterns: Fibonacci Numbers in Nature* make observation addictive. Read them once and then again. Then go to the garden and count petals or trace shapes. (Ask children to take pencil and pad or cameras along.)

Engineering Challenge

Build a garden! Using the practices of engineering, begin with data. When you have a plan, check and improve it. Ask children to talk to others in the learning community (especially custodians and cooks) and ask if their idea is practical, what problems the garden might have, and what will happen to the products of the garden.

Brainstorm all the things that make a garden happen. A class chart or board can help.

Begin with the soil. Bring soil into your learning space and examine it with hand lenses. Does it have big particles or small? Are there bits of living things in it? Soil that has more living things in it is more likely to be fertile.

Next, measure the sunlight. Instruments aren't necessary. Use the children's understandings from unit 9 to find places with shadows. If you used sunlight-reactive beads, you can use the data you gathered with them. Those are the places with the most sunlight.

How about intruders? Will your garden need a fence? Sometimes herbs can discourage small animals. You can discourage insects with a little soapy water (dish soap or shampoo) or small bits of soap around the edge of your garden.

Who will take care of the garden? Children are not at school all the time. With big calendars, identify the days help will be needed and ask families to come.

Where will the food go? Think about who might eat it. Can children help a charity?

Safety Note

Some soils (especially in cities) can be contaminated. Check your site's history. If there is any doubt, think about pot gardens, raised beds, or hanging gardens. Emphasize hand washing.

Content Background

The science of agricultural engineering includes ideas from both physical and life sciences. Novice gardeners soon discover that they must learn a lot, but the delicious results of that effort are well worth it.

The basis of any garden is photosynthesis. Plants need carbon dioxide, water, and sunlight. Through a complex series of chemical reactions, plants produce sugars and oxygen. Soil provides key minerals that are necessary for each of the chemical reactions. The most important minerals are nitrogen, phosphorus, potassium, and magnesium. While only tiny amounts are necessary, plants cannot live without them. The minerals also affect how acid or basic the soil is. For most plants, a very slightly acid pH (about 6.5) is best. The acidity is controlled by fertilizer.

The important STEM practice of arguing from evidence is well within the reach of a young gardener. Children can make observations about space, soil, sun, and water as they plan.

Safety Note

Toxins can remain in soil for a very long time. Where there might be any doubt about previous use of a potential garden site, have the soil tested. There are many options for pot gardens, raised beds, or hanging gardens.

Watch out for seeds treated with antifungal chemicals. Children should never handle them.

And, of course, all soil is potentially germy. This is a great chance to review hand washing.

- Gardens need safe spaces. They can't be planned in a place where people will trample them.

- The soil must be loose and fertile. Students can easily fix each of those components with tools, worms, and compost. Commercial fertilizers may be too strong. A lesson on building a compost bed is certainly appropriate.

- Plants have varied requirements for sun. Most seeds have notations on their packages that help with that choice. For example, tomatoes generally need a lot of sun; lettuce prefers shade.

- Include the children's outdoor time as part of your watering plan. Remember that well water may contain different minerals than rainwater.

Try It!

We will plan our garden by finding out how much sun, water, and space the plants will need.

Plant	Sun	Water	Space
Tomato	Lots of sun	Medium water	One-foot circle *(As big as a large pan lid)*
Pepper	High sun	Medium water	One-foot circle *(As big as a large pan lid)*
Radish	Medium sun	Medium water	Small circle *(As big as a saucepan lid)*
Lettuce	Low sun	High water	Many small plants will need a large area. One package of seeds might take up two square yards.
Carrots	Medium sun	Medium water	Small circle *(Each plant might take up one small saucepan lid.)*

Dear Families:

We are designing a garden! This activity will bring together all the ideas we have explored for many weeks in our STEM curriculum. We'll use science, technology, engineering, and mathematics to create a space where we can grow vegetables, flowers, and other sorts of plants.

Our garden will use the **energy** of the sun and the properties of water and soil. We will design the garden to make the most of our resources.

First, help your child observe gardens around your home and neighborhood. These don't have to be large or exotic. Pot gardens, roof gardens, and window plots are all examples of gardens within the reach of a young child.

Perhaps you can plant a few seeds at home. Pepper seeds (from the grocery store) grow well. Sprouts and herbs can be grown in almost any container to provide food for thought and for lunch!

Then follow our group gardening project with us. We will need a lot of help as we progress, and we would be very grateful for any supplies, time, or advice you can offer. (Grandparents and other helpers are welcome, too!)

Thanks for sharing your "flowers" with us. You are great STEM partners. Have fun.

From *Teaching STEM Literacy: A Constructivist Approach* by Juliana Texley and Ruth M. Ruud © 2018. Published by Redleaf Press, www.redleafpress.org. This page may be reproduced for classroom use only.

Be an Engineer!

Some engineers design gardens, forests, and farms. Agriculture is the science of farming.

Be an agricultural engineer. On a map of the yard, find a good place to put your group garden. Think about these things:

- sunlight
- rain
- wind
- people

Use the map you made with your ice cubes or sunlight beads to decide where to plant.

Some plants like lots of sun.

Some plants like a little shade.

Find some plants for the sunny spots near your school.

Find some plants for the shady spots near your school.

How will you get water to your plants?

_____

_____

_____

_____

_____

_____

_____

_____

(continued on next page)

(continued from previous page)

What animals might eat your plants? _____

_____

_____

_____

_____

How could you keep them out? _____

_____

_____

_____

Now think about these questions:

- What do you want to grow?
- Who will take care of the plants?
- What will you do with them when they grow?

Make a map of your garden here. Then ask a friend to help you improve it.

Carol Johnson: STEM Star

Carol Johnson is an architectural engineer. She uses earth materials and living things to create places people can enjoy.

Parks are fun for people of all ages. But some people have trouble moving around on grass, hills, or stony places.

Carol Johnson builds places for people who need extra help. Her parks and gardens have easy ways to pass through.

Think of the garden you planned. Could everyone enjoy it? _____

_____

_____

_____

_____

How could you make it better? _____

_____

_____

_____

_____

(your name)

STEM Star

You ask good questions!

You observe interesting things!

You solve problems.

When you don't succeed, you try again.

You never give up.

So you are a STEM star!

Make a list of all the things you can do:

_____

_____

_____

_____

_____

_____

Then do them.

Have fun!

The Last Word...but Not the End

One of the best aspects of integrating physical and earth sciences into early childhood education is the authenticity of children's investigations. The phenomena (in the terms of NGSS) that make children question and wonder are all around. They give children confidence in all areas of their lives.

We have written, read, and discussed other people who are STEM Stars. Now it's time to reaffirm children's capacities. Use the last STEM Star feature (page 156) as a certificate to congratulate children on something they have done well. Emphasize the times they have asked great questions, been innovative, used their own senses to find data for arguments, and, of course, taken paths you never expected or planned.

Don't stop with the ideas in this book. Opportunities abound for linking science to language arts, mathematics, and all other topics. The only barrier between children and these opportunities is the traditional bias that physical science and earth science topics must certainly be "rocket science." Of course they aren't! Anyone can explore them. The twelve units in this book should be only the beginning. Once you have tried these activities, you will probably change them to be more appropriate to your own group of children and to follow the curiosity of your learners. That's great. Start with STEM and enjoy the journey that follows. STEM is all about imagination.

In this spirit of imagination, we want to end this book with a thought experiment. Imagine that you are lazing poolside in the sun on a nice lounge chair. You have been resting for a long time, and it's very comfortable. But there's that great pool just a few feet away. It might be a little cool, might require you to wake up your muscles and challenge yourself a bit. It's tempting just to stay at the edge of the water. But swimming will take you farther and open up new possibilities. So you resist the impulse just to do what you've been doing. You get up and dive in. That's where the real fun begins.

Appendix A

Science Books for Children

Ajmera, Maya, and Dominique Browning. 2016. *Every Breath We Take: A Book about Air*. Watertown, MA: Charlesbridge.

Anholt, Laurence. 2007. *Leonardo and the Flying Boy: A Story about Leonardo da Vinci*. Hauppage, NY: Barron's Educational Series.

Barton, Chris. 2016. *Whoosh! Lonnie Johnson's Super-Soaking Stream of Inventions*. Watertown, MA: Charlesbridge.

Bradley, Kimberly Brubaker. 2005. *Forces Make Things Move*. New York: HarperCollins.

Branley, Franklyn. 2007. *Gravity Is a Mystery*. Toronto, ON: HarperCollins.

Brown, Jordan E. 2016. *Science of Fun Stuff: How Airplanes Get from Here . . . to There!* New York: Simon Spotlight.

Bucklin-Sporer, Arden, and Rachel Kathleen Pringle. 2010. *How to Grow a School Garden: A Complete Guide for Parents and Teachers*. Portland, OR: Timber Press.

Campbell, Sarah C. 2010. *Growing Patterns: Fibonacci Numbers in Nature*. Honesdale, PA: Boyds Mills Press.

———. 2014. *Mysterious Patterns: Finding Fractals in Nature*. Honesdale, PA: Boyds Mills Press.

Christensen, Bonnie. 2012. *I, Galileo*. New York: Knopf Books for Young Readers.

Cobb, Vicki. 2002. *I Get Wet*. New York: HarperCollins.

———. 2003. *I Face the Wind*. New York: HarperCollins.

———. 2004. *I Fall Down*. New York: HarperCollins.

DiSpezio, Michael A. 2006. *Awesome Experiments in Force and Motion*. New York: Sterling.

Ford, Gilbert. 2016. *The Marvelous Thing That Came from a Spring: The Accidental Invention of the Toy That Swept the Nation*. New York: Simon and Schuster.

Grey, Mini. 2009. *Egg Drop*. New York: Knopf Books for Young Readers.

Hollihan, Kerrie Logan. 2009. *Isaac Newton and Physics for Kids: His Life and Ideas with 21 Activities*. Chicago: Chicago Review Press.

Lai, Trevor. 2016. *Tomo Explores the World*. New York: Macmillan.

Lawrence, Ellen. 2016. *FUNdamental Experiments: Heat*. New York: Bearport Press.

Lendroth, Susan, 2014. *Old Manhattan Has Some Farms: E-I-E-I-Grow!* Watertown, MA: Charlesbridge.

Liukas, Linda. 2015. *Hello Ruby: Adventures in Coding*. New York: Macmillan.

Llewellyn, Claire. 2005. *And Everyone Shouted, "Pull!"* Minneapolis, MN: Picture Window Books.

Lowery, Lawrence F. 2014. *I Wonder Why? Dark as a Shadow*. Arlington, VA: National Science Teachers Association.

———. 2014. *I Wonder Why? Light and Color*. Arlington, VA: National Science Teachers Association.

Mason, Adrienne. 2005. *Move It! Motion, Forces, and You*. Mankato, MN: Kids Can Press.

Mayer, Lynne. 2010. *Newton and Me*. Mount Pleasant, SC: Arbordale Publishers.

Morgan, Emily. 2014. *Next Time You See a Maple Seed*. Arlington, VA: National Science Teachers Association.

———. 2013. *Next Time You See a Sunset*. Arlington, VA: National Science Teachers Association.

Murphy, Patricia J. 2002. *Push and Pull*. New York: Scholastic.

Nelson, Robin. 2004. *Push and Pull*. Minneapolis, MN: Lerner Publications.

Panchyk, Richard. 2005. *Galileo for Kids: His Life and Ideas with 25 Activities*. Chicago: Chicago Press Review.

Remenar, Kristen. 2015. *Groundhog's Dilemma*. Watertown, MA: Charlesbridge.

Reynolds, Paul A. 2014. *Sydney and Simon: Full Steam Ahead!* Watertown, MA: Charlesbridge.

Rich, Steve. 2014. *My School Yard Garden*. Arlington, VA: National Science Teachers Association.

Rosinsky, Natalie M. 2003. *Dirt: The Scoop on Soil*. Mankato, MN: Picture Window Books.

Sayre, April Pulley. 2015. *Raindrops Roll*. New York: Beach Lane Books.

Slade, Suzanne. 2015. *The Inventor's Secret: What Thomas Edison Told Henry Ford*. Watertown, MA: Charlesbridge.

Spires, Ashley. 2014. *The Most Magnificent Thing*. Tonawanda, NY: Kids Can Press.

Stewart, Melissa. 2014. *Feathers: Not Just for Flying*. Watertown, MA: Charlesbridge.

Stille, Darlene. 2004. *Motion: Push and Pull, Fast and Slow*. Mankato, MN: Picture Window Books.

Tomecek, Steve. 2016. *Dirtmeister's Nitty Gritty Planet Earth*. Washington, DC: National Geographic Children's Books.

VanCleave, Janice. 1991. *Physics for Every Kid: 101 Easy Experiments in Motion, Heat, Light, Machines, and Sound*. New York: John Wiley and Sons.

———. 2004. *Scientists through the Ages*. New York: John Wiley and Sons.

Vardell, Sylvia, and Janet Wong. 2015. *The Poetry of Science: The Poetry Friday Anthology for Science for Kids*. Princeton, NJ: Pomelo Books.

Weakland, Mark. 2014. *Thud! Wile E. Coyote Experiments with Forces and Motion*. Mankato, MN: Capstone Press.

Worthington, Michelle. 2015. *Noah Chases the Wind*. Saint Paul, MN: Redleaf Press.

Zoefeld, Kathleen Weidner. 2013. *What Is the World Made Of? All about Solids, Liquids, and Gases*. New York: Scholastic.

Appendix B

Web Resources for Children

10 Paper Airplanes

    www.10paperairplanes.com/how-to-make-paper-airplanes/03-the-arrow.html

Dirtmeister's Science Reporters

    http://teacher.scholastic.com/dirtrep/index.htm

Dynamics of Flight

    www.grc.nasa.gov/WWW/K-12/UEET/StudentSite/dynamicsofflight.html

How to Make a Dart Airplane

    www.grc.nasa.gov/www/k-12/Summer_Training/Elementary97/dart

The Land of Bump

    https://lob.concord.org

Sesame Street: Kermit and Grover: Hot and Cold

    www.youtube.com/watch?v=cqXSinx4-aU

Sunwise

    www.neefusa.org/sunwise

Teach Your Child to Make Paper Airplanes

    www.teachkidshow.com/teach-your-child-to-make-paper-airplanes

Toys in Space, 2

    www.youtube.com/watch?v=E9RDlIjgftI

Walking on the Moon

    www.youtube.com/watch?v=aQX9KOCS7MA

What Is Microgravity?

    https://www.nasa.gov/audience/foreducators/topnav/materials/listbytype/What_Is_Microgravity.html

Appendix C

Best STEM Books of 2016 for Young Readers

These books were drawn from the first annual list of Best STEM Books, a joint project of the National Science Teachers Association (NSTA) and the Children's Book Council (CBC). The list below is a selection of award winners appropriate to younger explorers. To see the complete list, go to www.nsta.org/publications /stembooks.

Barton, Chris. 2016. *Whoosh! Lonnie Johnson's Super-Soaking Stream of Inventions.* Watertown, MA: Charlesbridge.

Corey, Shana. 2016. *The Secret Subway.* New York: Schwartz and Wade.

DiOrio, Rana, and Emma D. Dryden. 2016. *What Does It Mean to Be an Entrepreneur?* San Francisco, CA: Little Pickle Press.

Drummond, Allan. 2016. *Green City.* New York: Macmillan.

Ford, Gilbert. 2016. *The Marvelous Thing That Came from a Spring: The Accidental Invention of the Toy That Swept the Nation.* New York: Simon and Schuster.

Lang, Heather. 2016. *Fearless Flyer: Ruth Law and Her Flying Machine.* Honesdale, PA: Calkins Creek.

Light, Steve. 2016. *Swap!* Somerville, MA: Candlewick Press.

Liukas, Linda. 2015. *Hello Ruby: Adventures in Coding.* New York: Macmillan.

Robinson, Fiona. 2016. *Ada's Ideas: The Story of Ada Lovelace, the World's First Computer Programmer.* New York: Abrams.

Rosenstock, Barb. 2014. *Ben Franklin's Big Splash: The Mostly True Story of His First Invention.* Honesdale, PA: Calkins Creek.

Scieszka, John. 1996. *The True Story of the Three Little Pigs.* London: Random House.

Slade, Suzanne. 2015. *The Inventor's Secret: What Thomas Edison Told Henry Ford.* Watertown, MA: Charlesbridge.

Spires, Ashley. 2014. *The Most Magnificent Thing.* Tonawanda, NY: Kids Can Press.

Stanley, Diane. 2016. *Ada Lovelace, Poet of Science: The First Computer Programmer.* New York: Simon and Schuster.

Appendix D

Resources for Teachers

Achieve, Inc. 2016. "Next Generation Science Standards." *Achieve*. www
.achieve.org/next-generation-science-standards.

Ashbrook, Peggy. 2016. *Science Learning in the Early Years: Activities for
PreK–2*. Arlington, VA: National Science Teachers Association.

Bransford, J. D., A. L. Brown, and R. R. Cocking, eds. 1999. *How People
Learn: Brain, Mind, Experience, and School*. Washington, DC: National
Academies Press.

Bybee, Rodger, Kirsten R. Daehler, Jennifer Folsom, and Mayumi Shinohara.
2012. *Making Sense of Science: Matter*. Arlington, VA: WestEd and NSTA
Press.

Bybee, Rodger, Joseph A. Taylor, April Gardner, Pamela Van Scotter, Janet
Carlson Powell, Anne Westbrook, and Nancy Landes. 2006. *The BSCS
5E Instructional Model: Origins, Effectiveness, and Applications*. Colorado
Springs: BSCS. www.bscs.org/sites/default/files/_legacy/BSCS_5E
_Instructional_Model-Executive_Summary_0.pdf.

Chalufour, Ingrid, and Karen Worth. 2004. *Building Structures with Young
Children: The Young Scientist Series*. Saint Paul, MN. Redleaf Press.

Common Core State Standards Initiative. 2016. *Common Core State Standards*. www.corestandards.org.

Discovering the NGSS. 2015. Arlington, VA: National Science Teachers
Association.

Fraser-Abder, Pamela. 2011. *Teaching Emerging Scientists: Fostering Scientific
Inquiry with Diverse Learners in Grades K–2*. Boston: Pearson.

Froschauer, Linda. 2012. *A Year of Inquiry*. Arlington, VA: National Science
Teachers Association.

———, ed. 2016. *Bringing STEM to the Elementary Classroom*. Arlington, VA:
National Science Teachers Association.

Goldberg, Rube. 2016. *Rube Goldberg*. www.rubegoldberg.com.

Keeley, Page. 2013. *Uncovering Student Ideas in Primary Science: 25 New Formative Assessment Probes for Grades K–2. Volume 1.* Arlington, VA: National Science Teachers Association.

National Association for the Education of Young Children (NAEYC). 2016. *Developmentally Appropriate Practice (DAP).* www.naeyc.org/DAP.

———. 2010. *Early Childhood Mathematics: Promoting Good Beginnings.* www.naeyc.org/files/naeyc/file/positions/psmath.pdf.

———. 2015. *NAEYC Early Childhood Program Standards and Accreditation Criteria and Guidance for Assessment.* www.naeyc.org/files/academy/file/AllCriteriaDocument.pdf.

National Council for the Social Studies (NCSS). 2010. *National Curriculum Standards for the Social Studies: Chapter 2—The Themes of Social Studies.* www.socialstudies.org/standards/strands.

National Institute for Early Education Research. 2012. *The State of Preschool 2012.* www.nieer.org/wp-content/uploads/2016/08/yearbook2012.pdf.

National Research Council (NRC). 2012. *A Framework for K–12 Science Education.* Washington, DC: National Academies Press. www.nap.edu/read/13165/chapter/1.

———. 2007. *Taking Science to School: Learning and Teaching Science in Grades K–8.* Washington, DC: National Academies Press.

National Science Teachers Association (NSTA). 2015. *Developing and Using Models of Electrical Interactions.* www.youtube.com/watch?v=BANW37RM6JM&list=PL2pHc_BEFW2KIK2maL8XW5gCIP1cpHH72&index=3.

———. 2014. *NSTA Position Statement: Early Childhood Science Education.* www.naeyc.org/files/naeyc/Early%20Childhood%20FINAL%20FINAL%201-30-14%20(1).pdf.

NGSS Lead States. 2013. *Next Generation Science Standards: For States, By States.* Washington, DC: National Academies Press.

Piagetian Interviews 1: Conservation of Mass. www.youtube.com/watch?v=wcdbkoInAeQ.

Piagetian Liquid Conservation Task. www.youtube.com/watch?v=h9ioMR8C9GI.

Ramirez, Ainissa. 2014. Address at the NSTA STEM conference in New Orleans. www.ainissaramirez.com.

Royce, Christine Anne, Emily Morgan, and Karen Ansberry. 2012. *Teaching Science through Trade Books.* Arlington, VA: National Science Teachers Association.

Stone-MacDonald, Angi, Kristen Wendell, Anne Douglas, and Mary Lu Love. 2015. *Engaging Young Engineers: Teaching Problem-Solving Skills through STEM.* Baltimore, MD: Paul H. Brooks Publishing Co.

Vardell, Sylvia, and Janet Wong. 2012. *The Poetry Friday Anthology (Common Core K-5 Edition): Poems for the School Year with Connections to the Common Core.* Princeton, NJ: Pomelo Books.

———. 2014. *The Poetry Friday Anthology for Science (Teacher's Edition): Poems for the School Year Integrating Science, Reading, and Language Arts.* Princeton, NJ: Pomelo Books.

WGBH. 2016. "Ramps." *Peep and the Big Wide World.* http://peepandthebig wideworld.com/en/educators/teaching-strategies/1/family-child-care -educators/2/learning-environments/17/ramps.

Appendix E

Selected Standards

Common Core State Standards for Mathematics Practice

1. Make sense of problems and persevere in solving them.

2. Reason abstractly and quantitatively.

3. Construct viable arguments and critique the reasoning of others.

4. Model with mathematics.

5. Use appropriate tools strategically.

6. Attend to precision.

7. Look for and make use of structure.

8. Look for and express regularity in repeated reasoning.

(CCSS Initiative. 2016b, 22)

Next Generation Science Standards

Scientific and Engineering Practices

1. Asking questions (for science) and defining problems (for engineering)

2. Developing and using models

3. Planning and carrying out investigations

4. Analyzing and interpreting data

5. Using mathematics and computational thinking

6. Constructing explanations (for science) and designing solutions (for engineering)

7. Engaging in argument from evidence

8. Obtaining, evaluating, and communicating information

Crosscutting Concepts

1. Patterns

2. Cause and effect: Mechanism and explanation

3. Scale, proportion, and quantity

4. Systems and system models

5. Energy and matter: Flows, cycles, and conservation

6. Structure and function

7. Stability and change

Selected Performance Expectations

Grade Band Endpoints for PS1.A

By the end of grade 2.

Different kinds of matter exist (e.g., wood, metal, water), and many of them can be either solid or liquid, depending on temperature. Matter can be described and classified by its observable properties (e.g., visual, aural, textural), by its uses, and by whether it occurs naturally or is manufactured. Different properties are suited to different purposes. A great variety of objects can be built up from a small set of pieces (e.g., blocks, construction sets). Objects or samples of a substance can be weighed, and their size can be described and measured. (Boundary: volume is introduced only for liquid measure.)

Grade Band Endpoints for PS1.B

By the end of grade 2.

Heating or cooling a substance may cause changes that can be observed. Sometimes these changes are reversible (e.g., melting and freezing), and sometimes they are not (e.g., baking a cake, burning fuel).

PS2.A

By the end of grade 2.

Objects pull or push each other when they collide or are connected. Pushes and pulls can have different strengths and directions. Pushing or pulling on an object can change the speed or direction of its motion and can start or stop it. An object sliding on a surface or sitting on a slope experiences a pull due to friction on the object due to the surface that opposes the object's motion.

Grade Band Endpoints for PS2.B

By the end of grade 2.

When objects touch or collide, they push on one another and can change motion or shape.

Grade Band Endpoints for PS2.C

By the end of grade 2.

Whether an object stays still or moves often depends on the effects of multiple pushes and pulls on it (e.g., multiple players trying to pull an object in different directions). It is useful to investigate what pushes and pulls keep something in place (e.g., a ball on a slope, a ladder leaning on a wall) as well as what makes something change or move.

Grade-Level Endpoints for PS3.B

By the end of grade 2.

Sunlight warms Earth's surface.

Grade Band Endpoints for PS3.C

By the end of grade 2.

A bigger push or pull makes things go faster. Faster speeds during a collision can cause a bigger change in shape of the colliding objects.

Grade Band Endpoints for PS3.D

By the end of grade 2.

When two objects rub against each other, this interaction is called friction. Friction between two surfaces can warm both of them (e.g., rubbing hands together). There are ways to reduce the friction between two objects.

Grade Band Endpoints for ESS2.A

By the end of grade 2.

Wind and water can change the shape of the land. The resulting landforms, together with the materials on the land, provide homes for living things.

Grade Band Endpoints for ESS2.B

By the end of grade 2.

Rocks, soils, and sand are present in most areas where plants and animals live. There may also be rivers, streams, lakes, and ponds. Maps show where things are located. One can map the shapes and kinds of land and water in any area.

Grade Band Endpoints for ESS2.C

By the end of grade 2.

Water is found in the ocean, rivers, lakes, and ponds. Water exists as solid ice and in liquid form. It carries soil and rocks from one place to another and determines the variety of life forms that can live in a particular location.

Grade Band Endpoints for ESS2.D

By the end of grade 2.

Weather is the combination of sunlight, wind, snow or rain, and temperature in a particular region at a particular time. People measure these conditions to describe and record the weather and to notice patterns over time.

Grade Band Endpoints for ETS2.A

By the end of grade 2.

People encounter questions about the natural world every day. There are many types of tools produced by engineering that can be used in science to help answer these questions through observation or measurement. Observations and measurements are also used in engineering to help test and refine design ideas.

(NGSS Lead States 2013)

References

Ajmera, Maya, and Dominique Browning. 2016. *Every Breath We Take: A Book about Air*. Watertown, MA: Charlesbridge.

Ashbrook, Peggy. 2016. *Science Learning in the Early Years: Activities for PreK–2*. Arlington, VA: NSTA Press.

Bybee, Rodger, Joseph A. Taylor, April Gardner, Pamela Van Scotter, Janet Carlson Powell, Anne Westbrook, and Nancy Landes. 2006. *The BSCS 5E Instructional Model: Origins, Effectiveness, and Applications*. Colorado Springs: BSCS. www.bscs.org/sites/default/files/_legacy/BSCS_5E _Instructional_Model-Executive_Summary_0.pdf.

CCSSI (Common Core State Standards Initiative). 2016a. "Common Core State Standards for English Language Arts and Literacy in History/Social Studies, Science, and Technical Subjects." Accessed November 21. www .corestandards.org/wp-content/uploads/ELA_Standards1.pdf.

———. 2016b. "Common Core State Standards for Mathematics." Accessed November 21. www.corestandards.org/wp-content/uploads/Math _Standards1.pdf.

Fraser-Abder, Pamela. 2011. *Teaching Emerging Scientists: Fostering Scientific Inquiry with Diverse Learners in Grades K–2*. Boston: Pearson.

Froschauer, Linda, ed. 2016. *Bringing STEM to the Elementary Classroom*. Arlington, VA: NSTA Press.

Launius, J. Carrie. 2017. Unpublished manuscript.

NAEYC (National Association for the Education of Young Children). 2015. "NAEYC Early Childhood Program Standards and Accreditation Criteria and Guidance for Assessment." www.naeyc.org/files/academy/file/All CriteriaDocument.pdf.

NCSS (National Council for the Social Studies). 2010. "National Curriculum Standards for Social Studies: Chapter 2—The Themes of Social Studies." www.socialstudies.org/standards/strands.

NGSS Lead States. 2013. *Next Generation Science Standards: For States, By States*. Washington, DC: National Academies Press.

NRC (National Research Council). 1996. *National Science Education Standards*. Washington, DC: National Academies Press.

———. 1999. *How People Learn: Brain, Mind, Experience, and School.* Expanded ed. Washington, DC: National Academies Press. http://nap .edu/9853.

———. 2011. *Successful K–12 STEM Education.* Washington, DC: National Academies Press. www.nap.edu/read/13158/chapter/5#18.

———. 2012. *A Framework for K–12 Science Education.* Washington, DC: National Academies Press. www.nap.edu/read/13165/chapter/1.

NSTA (National Science Teachers Association). 2014. "NSTA Position Statement: Early Childhood Education." www.naeyc.org/files/naeyc /Early%20Childhood%20FINAL%20FINAL%201-30-14%20(1).pdf.

Ramirez, Ainissa. 2014. Address at the NSTA STEM conference in New Orleans, www.ainissaramirez.com.

Stone-MacDonald, Angi, Kristen Wendell, Anne Douglas, and Mary Lu Love. 2015. *Engaging Young Engineers: Teaching Problem-Solving Skills through STEM.* Baltimore, MD: Paul H. Brooks Publishing Co.

Zoehfeld, Kathleen Weidner. 2013. *What Is the World Made Of? All about Solids, Liquids, and Gases.* New York: Scholastic.